C000259679

From

The 34 Great Sutton Street, London EC1V 0DX

Miranda Miller was born in London in 1950. She is the author of four novels, *Under the Rainbow* (Hutchinson 1978), *Family* (Hutchinson 1979), *Before Natasha* (Love Stories 1984) and *Smiles and the Millennium* (Virago 1987). Her collection of short stories, *A Thousand and One Coffee Mornings* was published by Peter Owen in 1989 and was nominated for the Macmillan Silver Pen Award. She is married, with one daughter.

Elaine Sheppard works for the Campaign for Homes in Central London, a federation of groups representing central London communities. She has previously been a community worker, and has studied social policy at the London School of Economics.

MIRANDA MILLER

Bed and Breakfast

Women and homelessness today

With an introduction by Elaine Sheppard
and an afterword by Sheila McKechnie,
Director of Shelter, National Campaign for the Homeless

The Women's Press

First published by The Women's Press Limited 1990
A member of the Namara Group
34 Great Sutton Street, London EC1V 0DX

British Library Cataloguing in Publication Data

Miller, Miranda
    Bed and breakfast: interviews about homelessness in London today.
    1. London. Homelessness
    363.5'1

    ISBN 0-7043-4204-9

Typeset by AKM Associates (UK) Ltd, Southall, London
Printed and bound by Cox & Wyman, Reading, Berks.

Contents

Acknowledgments

I should like to thank in particular all the people who allowed me to interview them about homelessness.

Thanks also to Judith Calvori, Sharon Convisser, Helen Crane, John Hall, Judith Hyman, Ahea Iqbal, Michael Miller, Vivienne Robb, Elaine Sar and Gerard Ward. Also my agent, Anne Dewe, Ros de Lanerolle at The Women's Press who took on what was then just a vague proposal for a book, and my editor, Hannah Kanter.

Author's note

Because of their vulnerability as a group, not wanting to compromise any of the homeless women, I decided not to use their surnames. In some cases pseudonyms have also been used. When I transcribed and edited the interviews, I cut my own questions unless I thought they contributed usefully. Most of the interviews are presented as monologues. The dialogues are in the main with the Tory politicians, in whose monologues I often intervened.

Preface

The idea for this book came out of my experience as a volunteer, working one day a week from 1987–8 in a toy library. I worked in a waiting room where people living in temporary accommodation in bed-and-breakfast hotels queue for advice, at the Bayswater Families Centre in Cleveland Square in West London. I was researching a sequel to my novel, *Smiles and the Millennium*, which had been set in the year 2000 in a London where the homeless live in shanty towns, disenfranchised, on UN rations.

I originally wanted to work in the toy library in order to see for myself what conditions were like for homeless people in contemporary London. As I talked to people living in the hotels, and to those who work with the homeless, the book in my head gradually became not a sequel to the novel but the voices of the people who had been telling me their stories.

I was shocked by the conditions they lived in, by the way they were bullied by hotel managers, and ignored both by the local authorities who were supposed to be responsible for them and by the Department of Health and Social Security (DHSS). I met children aged two or three who were obviously unhealthy. They could hardly talk at all and played with a terrible passivity. Most of their mothers were clearly depressed and run down, if not actually ill. Not all of them were like that; those who came with their children each day to the Drop-In Centre in the rooms next to where I worked were noticeably livelier. This made me feel the situation was not hopeless, and that individuals like those who ran the Drop-In Centre and the Families Centre could and did make a difference.

Talking to these women moved me and changed me. I began to think of them as 'us', not 'them', and to realise that homelessness could happen to me.

In this book I have tried to provide a forum for the views of many different women. Firstly, for homeless women, who have no political voice and whose stories are complex. Their interviews show that there is no such thing as a 'typical' homeless person. Secondly, for three politicians, all of whom have had experience of the housing policies of

1

the City of Westminster, the local authority area in which the bed-and-breakfast hotels described here are sited. Theresa Gorman, a Conservative MP, and Patricia Kirwan, a Westminster Conservative councillor, outline their views on housing. (Lady Porter, Chair of Westminster City Council, declined to be interviewed.) Jackie Rosenberg, a Westminster Labour councillor, explains why she thinks their policies are both callous and incompetent. Thirdly, I have interviewed four women who work with the homeless. They all know a great deal about the conditions in bed-and-breakfast hotels and the complicated problems of mental and physical health, education, violence and the threat of violence which are an inextricable part of homelessness. The women in this third group are struggling to help the homeless in London at a time when the Welfare State is being systematically destroyed by central Government.

Housing is a feminist issue: only one in ten households headed by a woman can afford to take out a mortgage. Two-thirds of the households living in bed-and-breakfast accommodation are headed by women. Women are more vulnerable to homlessness, as to other consequences of poverty, because they have lower incomes, and they will be even worse off under the new Housing Bill (now the Housing Act). Government housing policy since 1979, and the Housing Bill in particular, is enough to justify a belief that the government sees no future for women outside the family. 'Freedom to buy translates into the prison of an unhappy marriage, an overcrowded parental home, a bed-and-breakfast hotel or the streets.'[1] Women are told to stay at home, and are then denied a home. The family is sacred, but only if it can afford to offer expensive sacrifices to the money god.

My aim is to build up a picture of why people become homeless, how it feels to live in a bed-and-breakfast hotel and what could be done to improve the situation. I want to ask the following questions: What kind of capital do we want to live in – a city inhabited only by tourists and the very rich? Do people have the right to choose where they live? Does central government have an obligation to provide low-cost housing for those of its citizens who can't afford to buy or pay a 'market rent'?

My own answer to the last question is an unqualified 'yes', and this issue of citizenship is at the heart of my anger about homelessness. People who live in bed-and-breakfast hotels become non-citizens: it is extremely difficult for them to vote or to gain access to a GP or to find a school or playgroup for their children. When you become homeless, the first thing you lose is your privacy. Ginny had to go and live with her father-in-law who, she knew, had sexual designs on her. Deirdre and Jenny were subjected to sexual harassment and threats of physical violence. Shared bathrooms and toilets, inadequate shared kitchens and lack of play space all contribute to this lack of freedom. Almost every woman I spoke to compared living in bed and breakfast to prison, with the added stress that you are not told how long your sentence will be. As Dr Richard Stone, a local GP and Co-Chair of the Bayswater Project, wrote, 'Do people on low incomes have to be punished like this for not having enough money?'[2]

Although it is fashionable to argue that the kind of poverty described by Charles Dickens and Henry Mayhew no longer exists, I believe that Victorian squalor has in fact been restored, together with Victorian values. The government's 'trickle down' theory suggests that they seriously believe that a few thousand benevolent millionaires, grateful for the extra money they acquired in the 1988 Budget, will step forward and sweep up the debris left behind by the destruction of the Welfare State. This is reminiscent of the end of a Dickens novel. But Cheerybles are not thick on the ground in contemporary England, whereas Gradgrinds are flourishing on government grants.

I recorded most of these interviews during the first six months of 1988. With the exception of those with politicians, I tried to get to know the women a little before I interviewed them. Although those I have included do illustrate some general points about the housing crisis, these interviews stand above all as individual stories. These eight women's voices together do not amount to a representative cross-section of the homeless. I interviewed only women whom I met through the Bayswater Project, except in one case where a woman sought me out. In including among the eight two women who have had a heavy dependency on drugs in the past, I do not imply that the same proportion of homeless women have had a history of drug use.

Among the homeless women, many whom I wanted to interview disappeared before I could record their stories. People in the hotels can be, and frequently are, moved on at 24 hours' notice. Some homeless women were afraid of being interviewed in case they were thrown out as troublemakers. When I was trying to persuade a group of women in one hotel to attend a local meeting addressed by William Waldegrave, then Housing Minister, many refused because they were scared they would be thrown out of their hotel if they were seen at the meeting. One woman, Anne (whom I did not interview), who with her husband and their two children had been evicted from their Peabody Dwelling flat and had been in bed and breakfast for several months, did go to this meeting with her husband. The couple also gave an interview for a *World in Action* programme which was shown on TV. The family were in fact thrown out of their hotel. They were moved to another and eventually rehoused near Manchester, thanks to the efforts of the television company, which felt responsible for them. Ironically, I noticed that people who had the courage to protest – Anne and her husband for instance, and Doris, whose flat had been burnt out – seemed often to be rehoused more quickly than those who seemed passively to accept their situation.

Few women declined to be interviewed, and most who did were public figures. Some, like Mary Tester, were obviously restricted by their jobs. One administrator recorded an interview so bland that I knew I wouldn't be able to use it in the book. When I had switched off the tape recorder, she looked at me apologetically and explained that the government had made it clear they wouldn't fund any organisations that criticised their policies. The women living in the hotels speak much more frankly about themselves than the others. Although terribly vulnerable they spoke out of a sense of desperation and anger.

Many of the women I interviewed, particularly Ginny, Angela and Patricia Kirwan, expressed racist opinions. I have tried to edit these women's interviews in a way that neither denies their racism nor unnecessarily reproduces offensive views. Racism is widespread in the hotels. Some interviewees suggested hotels should be racially segregated. Although these women are all in the same situation, some of them find it necessary to cling to imaginary differences rather than band together to help each other. Instead of directing their anger where it belongs, at the government which has put them in slums, these women are blaming the disenfranchised for their own powerlessness.

Patricia Kirwan's views are more sinister because she has been powerful: as ex-Chair of Westminster City Council Housing Committee she had, as she boasts in her interview, more power than most MPs. She claims that many of the hotel owners are 'Bangladeshi themselves or Asian', although in fact the ownership of these hotels (which the government is encouraging businessmen to invest in) is extremely hard to pin down. Few readers will recognise Patricia Kirwan's England: 'the only country in the whole world that takes everybody who wants to come'.

With the exception of Doris, who is angry with central Government, the homeless interviewees tend to blame 'the Council' for their problems. This is a common argument which is worth examining in detail. As Jackie Rosenberg points out, local authorities are now so restricted by new legislation that it is extremely hard for them to spend money on renovating their decaying housing stock or on building new houses. The number of dwellings built by London councils and housing associations declined from 21,147 in 1978 to 2,490 in 1986.[3]

The Government has restricted the amount local authorities can borrow to build or renovate their property, and this figure has dropped from £1,975m in 1978–9 to £372m in 1988–9.[4]

Since 1979, under the Right-to-Buy scheme, London local authorities have sold over 90,000 council homes.[5] These of course tend to be the most desirable council properties in the area. So while local authorities are still obliged to rehouse large numbers of people, they have far less habitable property to do it in. The new Housing Bill proposes to transfer thousands of council properties to Housing Action Trusts (HATs) and to other private landlords with the prospect of higher 'market' rents. This will mean that although local authorities will still be responsible for rehousing homeless people, they will have even less property. For those who can't afford either a mortgage or a market rent, the outlook for housing in London is bleak indeed.

Numbers of households living in bed-and-breakfast accommodation in London have increased from 890 in 1981 to over 7,500 by the end of 1988. It makes more sense to blame Government policy for this increase than to rage at 'the Council', although of course many councils *are* inefficient. Margaret Thatcher's government wants to break the power of the local authorities, particularly in the inner cities where, as Theresa Gorman says in her interview, council tenants have traditionally voted Labour. Jackie Rosenberg believes that gerrymandering is a calculated part of housing policy in Westminster, where the Conservatives have a majority of only four on the City Council. It is, of course, extremely convenient for Conservatives to blame Labour ('Loony', as Patricia Kirwan calls them) councils for homelessness.

In 1988 the Association of Metropolitan Authorities estimated that it would cost £23 billion to repair the 85 per cent of council housing that needs work. Local authorities do not have that sort of money. Housing, like so much of our infrastructure, is rotting and I do not see who, apart from central government, can be held responsible for its reconstruction.

If my focus on Paddington/Bayswater seems parochial, I don't mean to suggest that what happens in Central London is more important than the housing crisis elsewhere. I concentrated on that area because I happened to be there, and found it more interesting to study a small area in depth than to approach the national homelessness crisis more superficially.

In 1988, 17 out of London's 33 local authorities placed 1,575 [6] homeless families and single people in about 120 bed-and-breakfast hotels in Bayswater. As well as being squalid, using bed-and-breakfast accommodation is expensive. Government figures in Hansard in

February 1989 showed that it then cost £14,600 to keep an average family in bed and breakfast for a year; financing the building of a new council flat cost £8,200 over the same period, the same as it cost to renovate an existing property. The concentration of homelessness in Bayswater is an historical accident; the hotels have been there for years because the area is central and attractive to tourists.

From the outside, most of these hotels look comfortable and have names suggestive of stately homes. Inside, many of them are slums. Overcrowded firetraps, they are infested with cockroaches, fleas, lice and rats. They have inadequate or non-existent play space, cooking and laundry facilities. It is so difficult to cook that most families end up living on takeaway meals, which are expensive as well as unhealthy. The bed or beds in the room usually have to serve as a sofa and table and chairs as well. In her interview, Helen describes how humiliated she felt when her little son asked why they didn't have a sofa like other people. Lavatories and bathrooms are usually dirty and shared by many people.

I heard many stories of bullying, threats and sexual harassment by hotel managers, who have appalling power over the lives of the people who live there. There is collusion between some of the managers and people who officially live in the hotels, but actually just come in once a week to 'sign' for seven days. One woman told me the manager had told her to pretend she had a baby, so that he could claim more money for her room. From a group of Bangladeshis, I heard about a housing official at Tower Hamlets who will only clear people as being 'genuinely' homeless if he is bribed. One reason why it is so difficult to count the people in the hotels is that it suits the managers to be vague about the exact numbers 'living' there.

The homeless in Bayswater, a shifting and demoralised group, are not organised. The only example I could find of a protest movement initiated by and for homeless people was the Tower Hamlets Homeless Families Campaign. The case of Bangladeshi homeless families, many of whom came to Westminster from Tower Hamlets, illustrates how rapidly the situation changes. In 1988 there were hundreds of Bangladeshi families living in Bayswater hotels. A year later most of them had been moved to Finsbury Park and areas of outer London. Of course the fact that the homeless are moved around like pawns, often to areas where they have no friends, makes it extremely hard for them to organise protests. Council tenants, however, do seem to have been galvanised into action by the threat of the new Housing Bill. The enterprising campaign organised by the tenants on Jackie Rosenberg's estate is one of many all over the country.

Another change which has taken place since 1988 is that London local authorities increasingly tend to use private rented accommodation rather than bed-and-breakfast hotels for homeless families. This saves the local authorities money, as the government subsidises most of the rent.[7] It is also less unpleasant for the families, as flats are at least self-contained and have their own cooking and washing facilities. However, they are only a temporary solution. Of the six women I interviewed who were living in bed-and-breakfast accommodation in 1988, only half (Ginny, Maria and Angela) had been permanently rehoused a year later. Families in private rented accommodation can still be moved on at very short notice, and homelessness is still increasing.

There are no reliable figures for how long it takes to be rehoused. People have stayed in bed and breakfast for anything between six months and four years. It is difficult to judge which boroughs are coping best with the situation; the answer would depend entirely on whether you asked homeless people or administrators, and on the political views of those questioned. As I have tried to show, people in the hotels come and go with bewildering rapidity and the situation changes all the time. This means that statistics about the homeless are difficult to collate and unlikely to be accurate.

One argument often used to show whether a council is 'good' or 'bad' at managing housing, is to count numbers of empty properties. For instance, in April 1987[8] there were 327 local authority dwellings in the City of Westminster which had been empty for more than six months. Of these, 107 were to be sold and only 10 were available for letting. Most of the others were either undergoing or awaiting repairs. These figures don't really tell us anything about Westminster's record on housing. As we know from Jackie Rosenberg, the Council has spent hundreds of thousands of pounds on vandalising its own empty properties and on expensive metal doors to keep squatters out. It was so anxious to deport its own homeless that it tried to build a shanty town in Barking, as Patricia Kirwan tells us. Even if there were a large number of properties in Westminster available for letting, it wouldn't help the homeless families in the hotels, nearly all of whom come from other boroughs.

The situation in the hotels would be even more explosive were it not for the work of the Bayswater Project. In February 1984 a co-ordinating group brought together local teachers, health visitors, doctors, residents, homeless families and church workers. They were horrified by the squalid and dangerous conditions people in the hotels were living in, and they agreed to meet regularly. Funds were raised to employ four full-time workers and two part-time people. They now organise two advice sessions a week, where families come with questions about housing, benefits, etc. Their problems are followed up. The Bayswater Project is funded mainly by the EEC (originally by the Greater London Council [GLC]), the Department of the Environment, the London boroughs of Camden and Brent, Shelter and SHAC (London Housing Aid Centre). The Drop-In Centre, run by Shelagh O'Brien and her colleagues for mothers and toddlers, is funded by National Children's Homes.

At monthly meetings, the Bayswater Project acts as an umbrella group for everyone in the area who is concerned about the problems of the homeless (including the homeless themselves), and as an information-exchange forum. Similar projects now exist in Earls Court and Finsbury Park, the other areas of London where there is a heavy concentration of bed-and-breakfast hotels used for temporary accommodation.

The work of the Bayswater Project is becoming increasingly difficult, at a time when its funding is coming under threat. From 10 April 1989, changes in Housing Benefit regulations now mean that families living in bed and breakfast receive even less money to live on. To give an example: before 10 April 1989, a couple with two dependent children aged 9 and 13 received £104.05 a week of which £86.80 was supposed to be for eating out at a calculated cost of £1.55 per person for each meal. This was an admission that cooking facilities in the hotels are inadequate or non-existent, but it does not of course reflect the actual cost of eating out. For some reason, the Government has now decided that people living in bed and breakfast have the same food needs as people in temporary flats, despite the fact that the second group *do* have their own cooking facilities. Since April 1989, our theoretical family of four now receive only £75.90 a week, altogether. Out of this they have to pay not only for lunch and dinner but also for breakfast, fuel, 20 per cent of their rates in the hotel and a proportion of their water rates. More and more adults and children will suffer from diseases related to malnutrition while the hoteliers continue to rake in their profits, with their rate and water bills conveniently reduced.

A recent report[9] quoted a health visitor as saying, 'If we are really committed to a healthy society we cannot allow homelessness.' Certainly conditions in bed-and-breakfast hotels make it almost impossible to stay clean and healthy. 'It is very difficult to keep things clean and sterile when you are washing and preparing food in the same sink that you have just washed a baby's nappy in.'

Predictably, 'In general women bear the major burden of hotel life and take the greatest responsibility for looking after children.' Out of

56 women in the study 44 said that they were 'unhappy most of the time'. The study concluded that bed-and-breakfast accommodation was particularly unsuitable for pregnant women. One woman living in a hotel said, 'I don't mind if I die, but if my baby dies what will I do?' Babies born to mothers living in bed and breakfast are far more likely to be underweight or sick at birth. 'Small, frail babies are less likely to survive pregnancy, more likely to suffer congenital handicaps, more susceptible to life threatening infections and less likely to enjoy a healthy childhood.' Over a third of the children in Bayswater hotels had behavioural problems.

Many 'hotel children' miss immunisation, according to the same study. In Hackney, out of a sample of 400 homeless children starting school at five, it was found that nearly half of them had not been immunised at all. A paediatrician said, 'You feel if there was an outbreak of polio or diphtheria it would whistle through the hotels.' Out of 39 women living in London hotels 14 had tried and failed to register with GPs. Many, like Angela, end up using the Emergency department at the local hospital. Some GPs do avoid taking on homeless families.

In Bayswater, three health visitors have to visit nearly 430 families. One midwife said she had to visit between 15 and 17 families a day. These figures are even more horrific when you realise that, of all the London boroughs, only Islington provides social workers with regular information on new families coming to live in the hotels. Health visitors have to knock on every door in every hotel to find out who is living there.

If life in the hotels is particularly dangerous for pregnant women, under-fives and their mothers, it isn't easy for older children either. They often have to share a bed with an adult or sibling. During the day, deprived of safe play space, they end up playing in the street or on roofs and other dangerous places.[10] In 1988 it was estimated that about 400 children in Westminster were without school places.

The most optimistic conclusion I can draw from all this is that protest does work. On an individual level, those like Doris who fought courageously may be rehoused quickly. At the level of local politics, the Tower Hamlets Homeless Families Campaign, which has survived for six years despite enormous difficulties, has provided roofs for many families who would otherwise be on the streets. Perhaps we can also learn from the enterprising campaign of the tenants on Jackie Rosenberg's Westminster estate. I hope that, as the housing crisis worsens, more and more people will unite in fighting government housing policies which threaten all of us. 'Sooner or later an election will be won by a party that offers a massive housing programme again.'[11]

9

Notes

1 Jenny Morris, *Guardian*, 26 January 1988.
2 *Speaking for Ourselves*, Bayswater Project, February 1987, £2.50.
3 Source: Housing and Construction Statistics 1976–1986, HMSO.
4 (Figures are adjusted to take account of inflation.) Source: Association of London Authorities, January 1988.
5 Source: Local Housing Statistics, HMSO.
6 Source: London Research Centre, Bed and Breakfast Information Exchange.
7 Funding varies from council to council, but local authorities do foot most of the bill for bed-and-breakfast accommodation. The DSS pays a contribution which was fixed in 1975, if someone is unemployed. For example, if a couple with a three-year-old child were living in a room in a bed-and-breakfast hotel costing £300 a week, the DSS would contribute £112.75, while the council would have to pay £187.25. The funding of private leased accommodation also varies. Generally speaking, the Government meets more than 75 per cent of the bill, which can be as high as the cost of bed-and-breakfast. The fact that this is a cheaper option for local authorities obviously encourages the spread of temporary schemes.
8 *Housing Needs and Resources in London*, London Research Centre, May 1988.
9 *Prescription for Poor Health*, London Food Commission, Maternity Alliance, SHAC and Shelter, 1988, £5.95.
10 *London Housing News*, February 1988.
11 Martin Pawley, *Guardian*, 8 June 1988.

Introduction
Elaine Sheppard

Homelessness and squalor are not terms which would be associated in many countries with hotels and bed-and-breakfast accommodation. In England today over 10,000 households, the majority headed by women, have nowhere else to live. It is salutary to remember that they are the fortunate among the homeless – their need for provision of some kind has been accepted. The more you find out about bed and breakfast the more shocked you feel that this is the solution on offer. That it is reflects a certain view of homelessness which we will see is not new. It is also the inevitable consequence of current housing policy. Both the attitudes and the policy seriously marginalise women's housing needs, with results which are illustrated most effectively – as they are in this book – in the words of women themselves.

More than 30,000 households are now living in temporary accommodation of different types, including bed and breakfast.[1] This represents a rapid increase since 1982 when there were just over 5,000. All are awaiting permanent housing by local authorities; some wait years. The total number of households accepted as homeless each year is now close to 120,000 (350,000 people).[2] Such statistics illustrate increasing *levels* of homelessness, while remaining quite inadequate as an indication of its overall *amount*.

The official figures only account for those whom local authorities take on a responsibility to house. Who they take on relates to their (limited) legal obligation, their attitude towards homeless people and the amount of accommodation and other resources available to them. Most homeless single people are currently excluded, and so are the many within the priority groups who fall into the 'intentionally homeless' category or who aren't judged to be homeless or 'enough' at risk. Those in the statistics are in bed and breakfast today in fulfillment of the duties of local authorities under the 1977 Housing (Homeless Persons') Act. A review of previous provision helps to put today's treatment of homeless people, and homeless women in particular, in perspective.

11

Deterrence: 'A secret known by all ratcatchers'

While the provision of 'indoor' and 'outdoor' relief for those in need has its roots in the Elizabethan Poor Law, it was the Poor Law Amendment Act (1834) that formalised the provision of shelter. Workhouses were established to keep the 'destitute' off the streets and casual wards were provided for those 'temporarily out of work and seeking employment'.[3] Their deterrent conditions and minimum provision were deliberately designed to put the principle of 'less eligibility' into effect. Those receiving help should be worse off than the lowest paid worker, or as it was put at the time, 'If paupers are miserable, paupers will decline in multitude. It is a secret known by all ratcatchers.'[4]

The principle is echoed clearly today, for example in the often expressed view that homeless people are 'queue jumpers' who ought to spend a minimum period of time in temporary accommodation and be grateful for any offer of somewhere permanent. Compare this description of the status of a 'pauper' given in evidence to the Royal Commission on the Poor Laws in 1905–6, with that of many bed and breakfast families today: '[Pauperism implies] . . . firstly the loss of personal reputation; secondly the loss of personal freedom, which is deterred by detention in a workhouse; and thirdly the loss of political freedom by suffering disenfranchisement.' The witness went on to say that there is in practice a right of relief, but this right 'is not a complete right for the necessary sanctions are lacking . . . he [sic] cannot sue for his relief'.[5]

Towards the end of the nineteenth century, under pressure from social reformers and more radical political ideas, the general category of 'pauper' began to be replaced with an acknowledgment of the specific needs of different groups of people (not including the homeless) – children, the elderly, the unemployed, the sick. The Royal Commission, which reported in 1909, recommended substantial modification of the principles of the 1834 Act.[6] Sydney and Beatrice Webb called for the end of the Poor Law and its replacement with a wide ranging system of public services administered by the local authorities. Despite supporting a more preventative approach, the main (Majority) report continued to categorise a residual group for whom the Poor Law Guardians would need to retain responsibility. Abandonment of the principle of deterrence was also accompanied by a continued concern not to be taken advantage of and even the Webbs advocated severe punishment of those who could be held to blame.[7]

This distinction between the 'deserving' and the 'non-deserving' was reflected in the first universal benefits – the provision, for example, of means of subsistence for the 'respectable' elderly poor who had worked all their lives (the old age pension), and insurance for those in employment. The criteria of deservability and respectability have continued to play an important role in the rationing of welfare state provision, including housing, and have had particular implications for women.

In a society which assumes the family to be the natural social unit, and women to be first wives and mothers, any contrary behaviour is certainly to be discouraged if not punished. While as primary carers of children women have also gained some access to assistance whatever their 'family status', this has been begrudgingly given – witness the blame attributed to single mothers today for the increase in homelessness.

Concerns about 'immoral' behaviour were close to the surface in the first state and voluntary sector intervention in housing in the second half of the nineteenth century. The huge influx of people into urban areas, seeking employment in expanding industry, had led to severe housing shortages and overcrowding. Some of the first legislation was to control standards in common lodging houses; of greatest concern to the Victorian middle and upper classes because of the threat that overcrowding and shared living arrangements posed to 'decent moral living and family life and ... to the ideal of the pure untainted Victorian woman'.[8] Watson and Austerberry illustrate the persistent preoccupation of the day with prostitution, reflected in the establishment by the Salvation Army and others of homes to restore in the women 'the highway of truth, virtue and religion'.[9] The first philanthropic housing provision, instituted by Octavia Hill in the 1860s, placed a strong emphasis on the guidance and tuition of the poor – in particular the encouragement of clean family living and high standards of housekeeping. Her early principles of housing management were to be very influential as local authority provision increased in limiting provision to the 'respectable', and in determining standards which were to be particularly severely applied to homeless people.

The Poor Law and its workhouse provision continued as a gap-filling service for the less deserving poor. Homeless people were no more than 'part of the confusion', with little attempt made 'to try and identify any group for whom homelessness was the main or only problem'.[10] It was not until the Second World War and the establishment of emergency feeding centres and temporary shelters for bomb victims that lack of shelter became an issue in its own right. In 1948 the National

13

Assistance Act put the first legal duty on local authorities to provide for the homeless, although – like wartime provision – this was limited to 'temporary accommodation' for those in urgent need. Provision was further defined as 'emergency shelter for victims of fire, flood or similar catastrophe' in response to 'need arising in circumstances which could not reasonably have been foreseen'. Although the severe post-war housing shortage ensured that demand escalated, a circular was swiftly issued to clarify that 'this provision is not one for dealing with the inadequately housed'.[11]

Homelessness was still viewed as a social rather than a housing problem. Provision was administered by welfare departments and was primarily in government rest-centres left over from the war. Ex-Poor Law institutions were also used and it is not surprising to find that treatment of the homeless reflected the same concerns about deterrence and training. Often only women and children were housed and many local authorities offered assistance for no more than a limited period, after which the children were taken into care.

Extra pressure tended to lead to more severe policies. A study of London homelessness in the 1950s found that families admitted to a night reception unit were required to reapply daily until investigations about rehousing were complete. Families in temporary housing were reviewed regularly to encourage them to find their own accommodation. The Ministry of Health in 1956 recommended training to help homeless people 'achieve an acceptable standard preparatory to rehousing'.[12]

The number of people accepted as homeless under the 1948 Act increased steadily. Although time limits and the use of institutional accommodation were increasingly discouraged by the Minister of Health, punitive views were still widespread. In the early 1970s Greve's London study found the general view among welfare departments to be that admission to temporary accommodation should not be too easy and that permanent rehousing should not be offered too quickly, if at all. A frequent distinction was made between those defined as having a 'genuine' housing problem and the 'wasters' and 'workshy'. Rehousing was also often dependent on 'standards of housekeeping and childcare [and] . . . good conduct' as well as rent paid up to date.[13]

By 1973 local authorities in London were already placing an average of 1,000 families a night in bed and breakfast for lack of other temporary accommodation.[14] Public pressure was mounting too; homelessness threatened a wider range of people and was generally being viewed more sympathetically. The poverty and homeless lobbies were becoming more powerful and in 1977 the government was finally persuaded to support new legislation with more teeth.

'A charter for scrimshankers and scroungers'

The Housing (Homeless Persons') Act placed new duties on local authorities, recognising homeless people as a distinct group whose problem required more than a temporary solution. According to one view expressed in 1978, the Act had 'laid the foundations for the construction of a basic human right – the provision of a decent, secure home for every family in the land'.[15] In a more recent legal judgment on the act Lord Justice Brightman pronounced: 'although the word "housing" is in the title it is not an Act which imposes on the local authority a duty to house the homeless. It is for the homeless a lifeline of last resort'. It is quite accurate to describe the Act as both extremely important and totally inadequate.

The 1977 Act forms the basis of statutory provision for homeless people today. It transferred responsibility from welfare to housing departments and required rehousing, not just a rehabilitation service. The Act extended legal rights to those threatened with homelessness as well as those already without a roof over their heads. It failed, however, by adopting of an all-too-familiar approach: to be simply homeless does not make you eligible; to qualify for assistance you have not only to be homeless or threatened with homelessness, but to fall within one of the strictly defined priority categories and be able to prove that you were not 'intentionally' homeless. You also have to establish a local connection to the authority to which you apply.

Local authority obligations are thus limited legally to the more 'deserving'. Families with children, pregnant women, those vulnerable through age, disease or handicap and those made homeless due to disaster (fire, flood) were made eligible by the Act. Those who could be deemed to be at fault, and able-bodied single people or couples who 'should' presumably not have a problem, were not. In practice, all elements of the equation are open to wide interpretation, and no legal force has been given to the accompanying and clarifying Code of Guidance. Homeless people have been given no right to appeal.

Opposition in Parliament to the bill as 'a charter for scrimshankers and scroungers' was an accurate indication of how some authorities would treat it in practice.[16] Homeless people are still subject to varying treatment – determined primarily by local authority attitudes, but increasingly also by the availability (or non-availability) of resources. All studies of the Act in practice show that much was unchanged by it.

The 'intentionality' and 'vulnerability' clauses have both been used to avoid responsibility for homelessness and homeless people are still treated differently from other housing applicants – for example in the type of accommodation they are offered.

A year after the Act a Shelter survey found that Slough was judging 30 per cent of its applicants intentionally homeless, in contrast to a national figure of 4 per cent. Purbeck council was erecting caravans for its homeless families, and bed and breakfast was often being used as a matter of course rather than 'as a last resort' as specified in the Code of Guidance. Homeless children were still being taken into care.[17]

A survey of London authorities in 1981 found that to be in rent arrears still meant designation as intentionally homeless. There were significant variations in the treatment of the young, the ill and the elderly. Only two boroughs accepted childless battered women (as recommended in the Guidance) and most insisted on injunctions having been granted, an attempt having been made to get a property settlement, and in some cases, visible signs of violence. Pregnant women were often not housed on the grounds that a miscarriage might make them no longer eligible. All boroughs surveyed made only one offer of permanent accommodation, in contrast to those rehoused from the housing waiting list. One borough admitted making deterrent offers to 'test genuineness', and one housed families directly into permanent accommodation only if it judged them 'suitable and capable'.[18]

A DOE survey of the Act in practice in 1986/7 shows that little has changed today.[19] To give but two additional examples, Wandsworth Council has recently stated that if a pregnant woman was accepted under the Act, 'the normal course would be a period of time in bed and breakfast, and then on to our reception centre prior to permanent rehousing being offered'.[20] In 1987 Westminster Council attempted to purchase land in Barking to erect Portacabins to house the homeless: totally inadequate temporary accommodation and many miles away from the local area of those people it was assisting. Such policies have, if anything, become more widespread as the housing crisis has forced authorities with more liberal interpretations of the Act to adopt a more severe approach.

Policies of deterrence are based on a view of homelessness as a residual problem which will only get out of hand by people 'taking advantage' of any assistance available. According to a recent housing minister, 'problems of affordability have become confined to a steadily narrower spectrum of the population and more and more to particular types of household'.[21] As emerges clearly from these interviews, homeless people are still widely thought of as 'queue jumpers', getting assistance at the expense of respectable local people who have waited quietly for years. They are 'young girls who get pregnant to get a council flat' or 'foreigners' – a 'problem' created by over-generous provision. It is clear that such views have always influenced the treatment of homeless people. They are now being used by the government to justify a review, and probable restriction, of current responsibilities for the homeless. How do they square with the evidence?

Official homelessness statistics show that there has been what the Audit Commission describes as 'a steady growth in the number of homeless households accepted by local authorities since 1970', despite wide variations in local practice.[22] Homelessness acceptances in London have doubled since 1978 and use of bed and breakfast has increased nearly four times.[23] In London alone, 75,000 homeless people were found to be sleeping rough or in hostels or bed and breakfast in April 1989, and much higher levels of 'hidden homelessness' have been clearly identified.[24] At the same time, households with children (the majority of those accepted as homeless) are actually falling as a proportion of the overall population. In 1988 an average of 86 per cent of homeless people had lived in the same borough for at least one year before becoming homeless, and the great majority were already on their council's waiting list.[25] Past peaks in homelessness (for example, post-war and in the late 1950s) have coincided with periods of housing shortage. The current downward trend in the accessibility of housing provides the only explanation for homelessness which is not shrouded in myth and prejudice.

Tory housing policy: the market will provide

State subsidy to housing provision commenced in earnest after the First World War, in recognition of the failure of the private sector to provide sufficient housing at rents affordable to those in need. The requirements of the economy for adequately housed workers, efforts to improve housing conditions through slum clearance, and the destruction of housing during the Second World War all played their part in establishing local authorities as major housing providers.

Labour and Conservative governments have hitherto differed only in the level of their support to council housing, and in the 1950s the Conservative government carried out a building programme to rival any Labour intervention. Council housing overtook private renting as the main source of provision for low-income households in the 1960s and was housing nearly one third of all households by 1979. However, owner-occupation also increased faster after the Second World War, and, with cutbacks in local authority spending since the early 1970s, it has been encouraged by both main parties as the predominant and 'natural' tenure.

Conservative housing policy, as it has developed since 1979, has followed certain basic principles. Firstly: the market is the natural and most efficient provider of all that anyone needs, including housing, and should not be interfered with. Deregulation could quickly revive the private rented sector, to meet the needs of all those people, for example the young and those requiring job mobility, for whom owner-occupation is not currently suitable. Secondly, owner-occupation (like marriage and a family) is the natural aspiration of all members of society and is the ideal form of housing. Thirdly, collective provision of housing by local authorities is the source of all evil. It is bad housing, unpopular and inefficiently run, and its provision encourages unhealthy dependency and reliance on the state and discourages individual responsibility. Housing associations (voluntary bodies) are better providers for the small number of people who will continue temporarily to require subsidised housing, but they should be made less dependent on the state and encouraged, like local authorities, to move towards 'market' rents.

The proportion of public expenditure going to housing has been cut from 10 per cent to 2 per cent since 1979, and local authorities are allowed to spend only a quarter of their previous allowance. As a result, the new building programme has collapsed: from over 100,000 completions nationally in the mid seventies, only 15,000 new houses were completed in 1988.[26] London has seen its new provision of council homes cut more dramatically than elsewhere, to less than 1500 units in 1988 – a drop of 94 per cent since 1977.[27]

The sale of council houses increased rapidly with the introduction of substantial discounts and the 'Right to Buy' in 1980 – such that the current council stock available for letting has now decreased by nearly one-fifth, well over a million dwellings.[28] The sale of whole estates to private developers and of empty flats on the private market has been encouraged. Hundreds of properties are empty and awaiting sale under Westminster Council's 'Building Stable Communities' policy for example, recently exposed by the BBC as a piece of social engineering to bring in more Tory votes.[29] As well as losing vital stock through the right to buy, local councils have been prevented from reinvesting the greater proportion of sale receipts.

Is this a rational policy to reduce 'dependency on the state' in the context of adequate private sector provision?

The private rented sector

Renting from the private sector has declined steadily throughout the century, from approximately 90 per cent of the housing stock in 1914 to 7.4 per cent in 1988.[30] London has retained a higher proportion of private renting, especially in certain central London boroughs, but its private rented sector is disappearing most rapidly. It is estimated that 750,000 lettings have been lost from the sector in London since 1961, and that it continues to decline by 17,000 lettings a year. It is mostly the older, secure and fair-rented lettings which are being lost, to more profitable conversion and sale into owner-occupation.[31]

Contrary to persistent Conservative party dogma, deregulation of rents and security have failed to revive the private rented sector. When such a policy was implemented in 1957, extra pressure on tenants only speeded up the loss of dwellings – the result was Rachmanism and increased homlessness.[32] 'Holiday' and 'company' lets, loopholes in the 1977 Rent Act, have ensured for many years that the vast majority of new tenancies are deregulated already. Neither they nor the less secure tenancies introduced in 1980 have stemmed the decline. Only the market for luxury letting, and in some areas letting to well-off professionals in shared housing, currently competes with the profits to be gained from conversion for sale and other forms of investment. To put the point simply, 'the rents demanded by landlords to persuade them to stay in letting are far beyond the means of the great majority of potential tenants'.[33]

Home ownership

'We in this country are extremely lucky to have a Government who run the economy in such a way that we can all afford to buy our homes,' said Edwina Currie MP in a recent parliamentary debate on housing.[34] Sixty-seven per cent of households in the UK own their own homes, but this is hardly proof that everyone can afford to and that everyone wants to, as the government would like to have us think.[35] Strong financial inducements to local authority tenants to buy their homes have been matched by a continuing huge subsidy to owner-occupiers in the form of Mortgage Interest Tax Relief. This has absorbed increasing levels of public expenditure to the detriment of rented housing and tenants. Now standing at £5,750 bn, it has for many years substantially exceeded the level of subsidy to council, housing association and private tenants combined (including capital subsidies and Housing Benefit).[36]

This subsidy to owner-occupation, and the benefits of a capital investment, have provided an enormous incentive. The benefits have been greatest for those on the highest incomes: the higher your tax bracket, the bigger your tax relief. It has also contributed to the escalation of house prices in recent years, which has only recently reached some kind of peak as lack of affordability has been compounded by increases in interest rates. A recent study for the Association of District Councils shows that the proportion of households who cannot even contemplate owner-occupation is increasing. This now applies to more than 50 per cent of households in 11 English counties, primarily in the South-East, and to more than 30 per cent in 26 further counties.[37] The average London house price is now £97,800, and it has been calculated that in 1988 nearly two-thirds of men and 90 per cent of women working full-time were unable to buy at £50,000 – the most 'rock bottom' price.[38]

Not surprisingly, reduced access to other tenures and the ready availability of mortgages has pushed more and more into owner-occupation who can barely afford it. Mortgage debt and repossessions have increased dramatically. Even before recent hikes in interest rates, 9 per cent of homeless acceptances outside London were previous home owners.[39] Reduced access to owner-occupation has also contributed to the decline in council houses available for letting, as the number of those who would normally move from council housing to owner-occupation has substantially diminished.

'Tenants' choice'?

The Housing Act which became law in November 1988 both consolidates these trends in Conservative housing policy and threatens to accelerate them dramatically. This is major new housing legislation which fails to mention homelessness and takes a head-in-the-sand approach to all other aspects of our current housing crisis. The Act ends fair rents and security of tenure for all new private tenants, putting housing associations, which have been designated the main 'social housing' providers of the future, in the same basket. New private rents are 'market rents', and although housing association rents are expected to remain 'affordable', 'affordable' has not been defined and subsidies to housing associations have been greatly reduced. Statutory rights, including the succession rights of current private tenants, have been taken away. In the crucial area of repossession, landlords can now evict more easily – for delays in paying rent, for rent arrears, and if substantial works (such as renovating a house to sell it off) are intended.

With the peak in Right to Buy sales apparently over, the Act has introduced other mechanisms to reduce the council sector. 'Tenants' choice' enables private landlords, including housing associations, to apply to take over council housing. It has been renamed 'pick a tenant' by tenants, partly in response to the controversial negative voting system which requires a majority of tenants on an estate to vote *against* the prospective landlord in order to prevent sale and counts non-votes as yes-votes.

Dressed up as a liberation for tenants from the 'dread drug of dependency' administered by local authorities, in reality the policy is more to do with Tory preoccupation with what are seen as strongholds of Labour voters – 'the evil empires of council housing'.[40] Where major repairs are required, the Act requires local authorities to pay costs to a new landlord on top of the loss of much-needed homes. Housing Action Trusts (HATs) are being set up on some large estates with the aim of selling off housing and bringing in different forms of management. United tenant opposition has led to the concession of a positive majority vote for HATs, and the only hope for the government now lies in the sizeable financial carrot on offer for repairs and improvements to those estates which 'opt out' in this way.

Low rents such as council housing are equated in government terminology with lack of 'individual responsibility'. The current Local Government and Housing Bill proposes to end local authority subsidy of rents and to push council rents further towards the market rents in their area. It also introduces further controls on capital expenditure; both measures which, it is hoped, will make transfer to another landlord more attractive to tenants.

Ministers claim that higher rents will attract increased Housing Benefit so there is nothing to worry about. In fact all they do is make more people dependent on a benefit which is regularly being cut back – eight times since 1983 according to Shelter.[41] Moreover, for the lowest paid the high cut-off point for Housing Benefit means that higher rents can require up to 60 per cent of income – before eligibility is reached.

A policy for homelessness

The effects of the 1988 Housing Act are only just being felt. Conservative housing policy was, however, already a policy for homelessness. The reduction in council housing in London alone is estimated to have cut lettings to new tenants from 47,600 a year in 1981 to 28,300 in 1988.[42] Nationally, a growing proportion of new lettings are now required to house homeless people accepted under the 1977 Act,[43] and in London the number of homeless acceptances each year has, since 1986/7, actually exceeded the number of new lettings available.[44] As a consequence, the use of temporary accommodation has increased rapidly, and a room in a bed-and-breakfast hotel is all that a large proportion of homeless households can expect as an initial, and increasingly long-term, response to their housing needs. At the end of 1987 there were 10,370 households in bed-and-breakfast accommodation, with 8,000 in London, and 2,000 of these in Bayswater.[45] Whilst inner London has the highest number of homeless acceptances these have for some years been increasing faster in the rest of the country. The use of bed and breakfast has increased most dramatically in recent years in the non-metropolitan south-east (by 80 per cent between 1986–7).[46]

The rise in bed and breakfast graphically illustrates the increasing levels of homelessness. It costs local authorities nearly twice as much to keep a family in bed and breakfast for a year as it would to pay the annual loan on a new council home.[47] Prevented from investing in new homes, London boroughs alone spent £99 million on this type of accommodation in 1987/8.[48] That this situation is tolerated reflects an extremely strong prejudice against the provision of new local authority housing, as well as a familiar willingness to perpetuate deterrent conditions for homeless people.

In 1989, the Government made life more difficult for those in bed and breakfast when it ended their eating-out allowance (which compensated for the lack of proper cooking facilities).[49] It also limited the scope of private sector leasing schemes through which local authorities and housing associations had started to provide homeless households with proper, if temporary, accommodation more cheaply than bed and breakfast. Some authorities have persisted with private leasing under the new, more restrictive rules, but it is notable that many others are apparently happy to retain the use of bed and breakfast, despite the higher cost.

There are a disproportionate number of both women and black people among those accepted as homeless, a reflection of a housing system which is increasingly geared towards ability to pay. Low income has become a major determinant of homelessness and under Thatcherism the number of those living below the poverty line has grown. Changes in Housing Benefit and the new system of income support have left poorer households worse off, and the poll tax threatens greater poverty. Those in low-paid jobs have also lost at a time when increases in house prices have risen twice as fast as increases in earnings.

As greater homelessness has been created, so the stigmatisation of homeless people has been accelerated. Little attempt is made to substantiate the many myths created to justify increasing levels of homelessness. In fact, official statistics show that 'over the past ten years, the recorded reasons for homelessness have changed remarkably little'.[50] The difference is that more and more people are affected. In all areas the highest proportion of households has been made homeless because of overcrowding – 56 per cent of households accepted in London in 1988 had been made homeless because of parents or friends being no longer able to accommodate them. Relationship breakdown is the next biggest cause, and although domestic violence is no longer recorded it is generally accepted that it is the reason for most homeless acceptances under this category. In non-metropolitan areas, private sector evictions accounted for 24 per cent of acceptances in 1988, and in all areas mortgage arrears are becoming a more significant factor.[51]

A restriction in the numbers of those for whom responsibility is accepted has been another inevitable response to accelerating homelessness in the context of reduced resources and the prevailing mythology about homeless people. The few authorities which had followed a more liberal line (in the spirit of the Homeless Persons' Act's Code of Guidance) have more recently abandoned such policies as the provision of housing for single women at risk of violence and non-use of the intentionality clause. The use of this clause has in fact increased, and black people and women have been among the first to suffer.

The London Borough of Tower Hamlets has adopted one of the more controversial interpretations of 'intentionality'. Following instructions to its legal department in 1987 to take a more 'rigorous view', the council evicted a large number of Bangladeshi families from bed-and-breakfast accommodation on the grounds that they had left accommodation in Bangladesh. The council evicted these families despite both their legal right to live and work in this country and lengthy periods of employment here by some household members. Such a policy has been found to be practised more covertly by other authorities, and has now been backed up by immigration legislation requiring wives and children legally joining their husbands in this country to show they can be housed and supported without recourse to public funds.

The increasing use of such accommodation as bed and breakfast and the appalling treatment of many homeless applicants has had its own significant effect in deterring applications. Pressure on homeless persons units has led to severely restricted services by some boroughs. In a couple of cases, the situation has been made virtually impossible for homeless people, with units closed so that contact could only be made by telephone. The accommodation of homeless families many miles outside their local borough has been a deliberate policy on the part of some local authorities with the aim of discouraging applicants.

The government's own response has been to develop perhaps the only alternative policy possible to the provision of more homes. Its much delayed 'review' of the homelessness legislation is widely expected to restrict the state's responsibility for homelessness even further. Perhaps homelessness will then disappear? A redefinition of homelessness as 'rooflessness' and a reversion to the provision of only temporary help are two new policies under discussion. A further suggestion is that the number of young women 'who get pregnant to jump the queue' should be minimised by the provision of 'hostel accommodation . . . which would house them properly, but would not be too attractive'.[52] The Conservative-controlled London Boroughs Association has joined many others in challenging this approach, warning that any change would 'exclude many people in desperate need' and that 'the shortage of decent housing available at prices within the means of potential customers' is the fundamental cause of homelessness.[53] The depressing fact is that the current Act has allowed so much scope for limiting provision to homeless people that the review will have to be dramatic to make the situation much worse in some local authority areas.

Women and homelessness: the double disadvantage

In line with the Government's preoccupation with 'morality' and 'family values', the above-mentioned focus on women as single parents reflects its fear of any policy which might be seen to threaten the traditional family unit. Such a fear has always affected women's rights. When women won the right to vote it was argued that this would lead to their neglect of 'husband, home and family'. One intention of early state intervention in housing was to curb supposedly wayward women and ever since, housing policy has both reflected and reinforced family ideology.

However, the exclusive focus of Tory policy on owner-occupation now makes homelessness, and particularly homelessness for women who do not conform to the family stereotype, more inevitable than it has been. At best it restricts women's choices. At worst, as the interviews show, it endangers their very lives. Women are made out to be at fault in order to pave the way for reducing provision yet further. What they already put up with – bed and breakfast, night shelters, the streets – is surely proof enough that there is nowhere else for them to go.

Current housing policy has quite distinct implications for different sections of society. Women themselves have been affected differently according to their class, their colour, their physical ability, their sexuality, their age and many other differences in their lives. When referring to women's experience in general it is essential to bear in mind that many women are at least doubly disadvantaged when it comes to housing and homelessness.

Women's average full-time earnings in 1989 were still well below men's. Those in non-manual jobs took home only 61 per cent of average male earnings, a situation which has actually deteriorated since the 1975 Equal Pay Act.[54] Their economic position stems from the sexual division of labour which continues so successfully to meet the needs of our patriarchal and capitalist society. At home, women take primary responsibility for caring for children, for dependent relatives and for housework. The majority of working-age women work outside the home too. However, their home responsibilities and the lack of childcare provision confines the majority to 'women's jobs', low-paid and part-time, and increasingly in the service sector. Their economic dependence on men and their inferior standing in society contributes strongly to women's experience of violence and abuse, in the home and outside it. It also affects their health – marriage and motherhood have been found to make women much more prone to depression than either married men or single women.[55]

The tax and social security systems, like housing policy, still largely assume that women live with husbands and have children. Their work as wives and mothers is natural and requires no compensation. Long-standing changes in household formation – whereby the model of two parents with dependent children has steadily reduced to less than 30 per cent of households today – are still not adequately acknowledged.[56] The consequence is that many women are very poor. Single parents, 90 per cent of whom are women, are stuck in a poverty trap – unable to work because of lack of childcare provision, and losing nearly all benefit if they do attempt to. The freezing of child benefit, cuts in social security benefits, reduced nursery provision, and community care policies which depend on women as the carers have all in recent years further undermined any hope of independence for many women. The latest proposal (from both sides of the political spectrum) to reduce benefits to single parents by requiring absent fathers to pay more in maintenance, epitomises the current trend.[57] It is a trend which makes women more, not less, economically dependent on men, and discourages departure from the family form.

Housing for families or housing for women?
The studies of women and housing which have been carried out (still too few) emphasise the role housing has played in reinforcing women's oppression. Arguably, it has never favoured women as independent beings either in its design or its accessibility. As Watson and Austerberry ably illustrate, 'British housing policy and the housing market operate in favour of the traditional nuclear family household ... [and] this dominant family model assumes a domestic role for women'.[58]

The post-war Labour government stated in 1946 that 'the Government's first objective is to afford a separate dwelling for every family which desires to have one'. In 1971 owner-occupation was given the full backing of the Conservative Party on the grounds that 'it satisfies a deep and natural desire on the part of the householder to have independent control of the house that shelters him and his family'.[59] Although the form of state intervention in housing has varied throughout the century it has not wavered in its almost exclusive concern with *family* housing. Described by Geoffrey Howe MP as 'the central unit of a stable society', the privatised family – in which children are cared for and socialised and workers are provided for cheaply and supported emotionally – has provided an essential prop to the capitalist system. State intervention in the provision of housing responded to economic, equated with family, needs.

The preoccupation with family was explicit in early designs for the philanthropic 'model dwellings' which stressed the 'preservation of domestic privacy and the independence of each distinct family', and had strict rules about 'respectable behaviour' and keeping out non-family lodgers.[60] Housing design has also reflected clear ideas about the role and status of women, with the parlour or kitchen often at the back and of a size to prevent more than one person working. The inter-war expansion of owner-occupation to the middle classes took the form of the 1930s 'semi' with its image of privacy and correctness. Council housing has been almost exclusively family housing with any provision for single people described as 'special needs' as opposed to 'general needs' housing.

Since the 1950s, both Conservative and Labour governments have encouraged owner-occupation as the main tenure to meet housing needs. Home ownership in practice is far from a 'natural' form of housing for women. It is expensive, carries potentially onerous maintenance responsibilities and has little flexibility to changing circumstances. Whilst mortgage companies less frequently refuse mortgages to single women than they did, owner-occupation is ever more reliant on high incomes – in most cases, two incomes. The 1984 General Household Survey found that only 11 per cent of woman-headed households were owner-occupiers currently paying a mortgage, compared with 42 per cent who held local authority tenancies.[61] Access for women to owner-occupation has been determined by a relationship with a man, more so than for any other kind of accommodation.

Council housing was originally housing for 'respectable' working families and its allocation has in many instances discriminated against others such as single parents and black people. However, the affordability of council rents has made it an extremely important source of housing for some women, divorce and separation having left many as heads of households in the council sector. Council housing has also generally moved towards allocation according to greatest housing need (irrespective of family status), in relation to households with children. In practice, the increase in the proportion of council lettings to those accepted under the Homeless Persons' Act has *improved* access to some woman-headed households in the most desperate circumstances. Some local authorities have in recent years developed more progressive policies to deal with relationship breakdown, domestic violence, racial harrassment and, in some cases, the needs of lesbian and gay couples with children. Although these have suffered with expenditure cuts, the fact remains that local authorities and housing associations are the only providers of housing likely to have such policies (or be affected by outside pressure to adopt them). Single women and adult households without children are currently far less likely to be housed unless elderly or otherwise 'vulnerable'.

The private rented sector has been 'the major source of accommodation for the non-nuclear family household in need of housing'.[62] It is in practice the only current source of housing for non-'vulnerable' single women who cannot afford owner-occupation. It has also provided some scope for other groups excluded from council housing. However, it is a dwindling sector, already inaccessible to many. Higher rents and less security threaten to limit its role even further, and substantially to worsen the conditions faced by those who currently rely on it.

It has already been found that women are more than twice as likely as men to suffer harassment and poor living conditions in the private rented sector.[63] This is particularly so for black women, migrant women and lesbians, and a high proportion of current private tenants are some of the most vulnerable – elderly women living on their own. Prejudice has often excluded women with children, as well as other groups, from private renting. Rent levels in the private rented sector have for many years made it inaccessible to those on low incomes. This has been exacerbated by benefit changes in the 1988 Social Security Act and it looks likely that the benefit limits to be set by rent officers under the new Housing Act will be much lower than landlords will want to charge.

Housing associations were originally seen as the major providers of housing for single people. In practice they have primarily provided for those with 'special needs'; the elderly, the disabled, the mentally ill and handicapped and some other single homeless people. In recent years they have housed more homeless families through local authority nominations, and the current intention that housing associations should become primary providers of new 'social housing' makes it likely that they will play a larger role in housing the priority homeless at the further expense of single people.

The new financial regime for housing associations is also likely to have the effect of limiting the few initiatives (for example in provision for single working women) which have benefited women without children. Co-ops, including women-only co-ops, have had a small but important role in housing women on low incomes and are under threat from the same new regime and a reduction in the availability of short-life accommodation.

Social housing

'A second class sector'

Council and housing association provision has been most suited to women's needs. Unfortunately it has not been accessible to all women, and unless there is a dramatic reversal in current trends it will tend to become even less so. Resources for housing associations are increasing, but at the direct expense of further reductions in local authority expenditure. New housing association provision will certainly not be adequate to meet the ever-growing needs of new households as well as to compensate for the further decline in council housing.

Council housing, (and by implication housing association housing – already widely dubbed 'social housing'), has been designated by a Tory party think-tank as 'only . . . for those who whether through poverty or lack of initiative cannot make the grade as owner occupiers. We've got to accept it is a second-class sector for second-class people.'[64] Little more needs to be said to illustrate the marginalisation of women's needs by current policy.

The prospects for women who do not meet the neat stereotype of success in capitalist and patriarchal terms (marriage, family and enough wealth to afford owner-occupation) are grim. Those whose rehousing needs continue to be recognised will face longer waits in inadequate temporary accommodation for welfare-style housing. Higher rents will condemn many more to dependence on benefits, the only council housing left will be the least popular (which has not been sold under the Right to Buy), and any new housing association provision will be in the cheapest areas with little regard to the community networks on which women are particularly reliant. Bed-and-breakfast conditions may only be a taster for future permanent rehousing options. These interviews illustrate the toll on women's physical and mental health this would represent.

The future role of housing associations in housing women without children, even those with 'special needs', must be in doubt. The prospects for single women and couples without children, many of whom of course have no greater ability to house themselves in the private sector, are worse than ever before.

One of the desired effects of cutting state provision and deterring demand is to keep women in what is deemed to be their proper place – at home as half of a respectable 'happy' couple, dependent on a mythically provident husband to support their housing needs. It will inevitably succeed to some extent – as the deterrent conditions of bed and breakfast have already ensured. However, the aim does not respond to the realities of a large number of women's lives, and the policy does not match the realities of the housing market or, any more, the needs of the economy. Adult-only households and woman-headed households have been increasing for many years. The incidence of divorce alone multiplied seven times between 1962–1981, and by 1987 over 30 per cent of London's households were headed by women and 19 per cent of families were single-parent families.[65]

Some women have chosen positively against 'the family' and against heterosexuality, many women have been left on their own through family break-up, and many others have been physically and mentally hurt in the family structure – through domestic violence and sexual abuse as children. Women's refuges, set up in the early 1970s, provided evidence to challenge the myth of women's safety in the family home; ' "home" for men was not the same as home for women'.[66] In London, 100,000 women every year now need medical treatment because of battering at home.[67] One survey carried out in women's refuges found that 32 per cent of the women had not been accepted as homeless for reasons including lack of evidence of battering (couldn't show the bruises) and the fact that that they had a home in the refuge.[68] Even so, in metropolitan areas outside London 26 per cent of homeless acceptances in 1981 were women seeking housing because of marital relationship breakdown, and the vast majority of them were fleeing domestic violence.[69] Our housing policy is already condemning women to violent relationships in the absence of any other option, and those who get help are often placed in notoriously insecure bed-and-breakfast accommodation.

Women need independent access to housing they can afford for reasons of life and death as well as choice. They are not a marginal group with unusual needs but a majority of the population whose access to housing is denied by policies which promote owner-occupation at the expense of all other forms of housing. Perhaps the twin facts that it is increasingly difficult to describe owner-occupation as affordable to the majority and that the economy is suffering (particularly in the South-East) from labour shortages related to the lack of access to housing make it more hopeful that some women's needs will be met.

However, housing policy must recognise the needs and differing aspirations of women in their own right if it is going to mean anything but homelessness for such a high number. It is currently being used to turn back the clock and reinforce women's oppression. Increasing numbers of women do not fit the stereotype as part of the 'successful' property-owning family. They are forced to make do in situations of overcrowding, bad conditions and often abuse. Those for whom some provision in legislation has been made are still, in the best poor law tradition, likely to be viewed as inadequate and in need of special help or training. At worst (and more often) they are seen as blameworthy and deserving of minimal, and hopefully deterrent, provision.

Bed-and-breakfast conditions are still tolerated in the hope that our independence as women – an independence we have a right to and an independence we need – will somehow go away. Now more than ever, feminists need to push housing higher up the political agenda.

Notes

1   *Housing the Homeless: the Local Authority Role*, Audit Commission, 1989 p.10. Unless otherwise stated all statistics are for England alone. Many other households, including single people, place

themselves in bed-and-breakfast accommodation, although benefit changes since 1985 have made this more difficult.

2 Booth, A. *Raising the Roof on Housing Myths*, Shelter, 1989, p.43.
3 Watson, S. and Austerberry, H., *Housing and Homelessness: A Feminist Perspective*, Routledge and Kegan Paul, 1986, p.31.
4 B. Glastonbury, *Homeless near 1000 Homes: a study of families without homes in South Wales and the West of England*, Allen and Unwin, 1971, p.27: Statement by Thomas Carlyle.
5 Rees, A.M., *T.H. Marshall's Social Policy*, Hutchinson, 1985, p.26.
6 ibid., p.44.
7 ibid., pp.44–50.
8 Watson S. and Austerberry, H., op.cit., pp.27–33.
9 ibid., p.36.
10 Glastonbury, B., op.cit., p.33.
11 Greve, J., *Homelessness in London*, Scottish Academic Press, 1971, p.124.
12 ibid., p.125.
13 ibid., p.149.
14 Bailey, R., *The Homeless and the Empty Houses*, Penguin, 1977.
15 *Where Homelessness means Hopelessness: an appraisal of the first year of the Housing (Homeless Persons') Act*, compiled by S. Billcliffe, Shelter, 1978, p.2.
16 Donnison, D. and Ungerson, C., *Housing Policy*, Penguin, 1982, p.275.
17 Billcliffe, S., op.cit., p.4.
18 Goss, S., *Working the Act: The Homeless Persons' Act in Practice*, SHAC, 1983.
19 Evans, A. and Duncan, S., *Responding to Homelessness: Local Authority Policy and Practice*, Department of the Environment, 1988.
20 *Speaking Out*, Report of the London Housing Inquiry, London Housing Forum, 1988, p.78.
21 Speech by the Earl of Caithness, to the US/UK Conference on Affordable Housing, July 1989.
22 Audit Commission, op.cit., p.9.
23 *Homelessness and Housing Need in London*, London Research Centre, June 1989, p.1.
24 Salvation Army Survey, reported in the *Guardian*, 28 July 1989.
25 'What's Causing Rising Family Homelessness?', Bayswater Homelessness Project, August 1989; see also *Giving Hope to London's Homeless – The Way Forward*, London Boroughs Association, May 1989, p.29.

26 Booth, A., op.cit., p.49.

27 London Boroughs Association, op.cit., p.7.

28 Murie, A., Paper to 'Housing the Community in Greenwich' Conference, September 1989.

29 Panorama Programme, BBC, 19 July 1989.

30 London Boroughs Association, op.cit., p.7.

31 *Homelessness in London*, Association of London Authorities, November 1988

32 Balchin, P., *Housing Policy: An Introduction*, Croom Helme, 1985, p.102.

33 Burrows, L., *The Housing Act 1988*, Shelter, 1989, p.10.

34 Hansard, Report of House of Commons proceedings, 2 March 1989.

35 Booth, A., op.cit., p.17.

36 Crofton, B., Paper to 'More than a Roof: the future for social housing', conference organised by Roof and Ealing Family Housing Association, March 1989.

37 *Access to Owner Occupation – Update to 1989*, Association of District Councils.

38 London Research Centre, op.cit., p.7.

39 Audit Commission, op.cit., p.9.

40 Quotes from William Waldegrave MP, then Housing Minister, and and Bob Hughes MP.

41 Shelter, Housing Monitor, October 1987.

42 *Homelessness in London*, op.cit.

43 Audit commission, op.cit., p.17.

44 *Homelessness in London*, op.cit.

45 *Who Will House The Homeless*, Institute of Housing, Autumn 1988, p.37; Audit Commission, op.cit., p.12; Bayswater Hotel Homelessness Project, newsletter, April 1989.

46 Institute of Housing, op.cit., p.9.

47 London Research Centre, op.cit., p.2.

48 *Homelessness in London*, op.cit.

49 'Enough Money to Eat?', Shepherds Bush Families Centre et al, March 1989.

50 Audit Commission, op.cit., p.14.

51 ibid.

52 'Whitehall sources' quoted in the *Observer*, 14 April 1989.

53 London Boroughs Association, op.cit.

54 *Women and Men in Britain, 1989*, Equal Opportunities Commission. Female manual employees receive 72 per cent of average male pay.

55 Research into the effects of parenthood, by Birmingham University, quoted in *Daily Mail*, 2 Sept.1989.

56 Watson, S., 'Housing and the Family: the marginalisation of non-family households', Journal of Critical Social Policy, 1984.

57 Report of Panorama Programme in the *Guardian*, 18 Sept.1989. New report by Frank Field MP, the *Guardian*, 14 Sept. 1989.

58 Watson, S. and Austerberry, H., op.cit., pp. 3-4.

59 ibid., p.49.

60 Matrix, *Making Space: Women and the Built Environment*, Pluto Press, 1984, p.63.

61 *The Impact on Women of National Housing Policy since 1979*, Shelter, December 1987, p. 3.

62 Watson, S. and Austerberry, H., op.cit., p. 16.

63 Bates, F., Paper to Shelter 'Women and the Housing Bill' conference, January 1988.

64 Quoted in background paper to 'More than a Roof: The future for social housing' conference, p.6.

65 Watson., S. and Austerberry H., op.cit., p.6; see also *London Women into the 1980s*, London Strategic Policy Group, 1987, p.19.

66 Roberts, M., 'Women and Housing: An Overview', Women and the Built Environment, issue 11, p.3.

67 Whyte, Alison, 'At home with fear', Roof, July-Aug. 1989, p.11.

68 Binney, V., Harkell G., and Nixon, J., *A Study of Refuges and Housing for Battered Women*, Women's Aid Federation, 1981.

69 'What's Causing Rising Family Homelessness?', op.cit.

PART ONE

Interviews with homeless women

It is a sobering thought that those who are given temporary accommodation in hotels are the privileged minority (36 per cent) of London's homeless.

In their pamphlet *Speaking for Ourselves* the Bayswater Project give a rough breakdown of why people find themselves in bed and breakfast, having been accepted as 'genuinely homeless' by a London local authority: 50 per cent are homeless because parents, relatives or friends can no longer accommodate them; 9 per cent, including a growing number of elderly single people, have been evicted from privately rented homes; 12 per cent are women who have fled domestic violence. Of the remaining 29 per cent, many become homeless because of mortgage default, which is now increasing very rapidly as interest rates rise. Another cause of homelessness is reduced funding of the National Health Service; bed-and-breakfast hotels are used as a way of dumping people released from psychiatric hospitals and prisons under the 'Community Care' scheme. Having discovered that the community doesn't care, single people, who may be extremely disturbed, spend long periods isolated in the hotels.

What such figures can't communicate is the suffering of people living in the hotels. I was shocked by the number of references to violence, suicide and sexual harassment in these interviews. Marriages and relationships break down and children – like Deirdre's daughter – are taken into care because of the unbearable pressures of hotel life. Small children – like Angela's son – develop health problems which almost certainly would not have occurred if they had been living in a stable home on a healthy diet. People in the hotels are far more vulnerable to accidents – fires, falls, scalds from kettles and dangerous cooking facilities – as well as to every kind of mental and physical illness. The temptation to use drugs or alcohol to block out an intolerable reality is described by Maria, Ginny and Jenny.

Angela

I met Angela when she came to the toy library with her baby son, Adam. They had been living in bed and breakfast for ten months, since just after Adam was born. Angela has been married twice and has two daughters by her first marriage, both of whom are in foster care. She used to work as a barmaid but was unemployed at the time of this interview. She is a tall, sturdy woman of 34. Her story shows how little protection women have against domestic violence. Her son's history of bad health is typical of small children living in the hotels: overcrowded conditions and inadequate food and hygiene cause problems which become serious because the children and their mothers have no GP and, often, no health visitor either.

As I listened to Angela's account of her own and her daughter's sexual abuse I kept wondering if I should switch the tape recorder off. But Angela wanted to go on talking. Of all the voices in this book, hers is the one I can still hear most vividly; a strong, heartbroken, London voice.

I left my husband. I had a flat in Putney. I left him because he started to become violent. He burst my eardrum, and I had to go to the hospital and they wanted to take a police action out on him. I'd been with him about ten years, married about four. Finally, I couldn't stand any more, so I left him. I went to live in where I used to work, as a barmaid. I met another fellow, and we started to go out with each other. Then I found I was pregnant and that fellow didn't want to know me: so not only am I pregnant now, but I haven't got a job. So I moved in with my sister. And my sister couldn't put up with me; she only had a two-bedroom flat. She's got two children of her own. There was her and her boyfriend, she was pregnant again, and she had my mum living with her. So it was a great strain to live with my sister. Well, in the end I went along to Lewisham Council. Lewisham said they wasn't taking any responsibility, that I should be under Wandsworth. So I've been in bed and breakfast now a year, and still Lewisham haven't notified me about what they're doing. So now I've put in an ombudsman's complaint.

When I very first went into bed and breakfast, they stuck me up 72 stairs with a baby and a buggy and shopping. I was in a tiny little room which wasn't even six foot by eight foot. After many months of complaining, they moved me across the landing to a bigger room. But then they obviously wanted that bigger room for a family, so they moved me right downstairs to the basement. It wasn't too bad, apart from people chucking dirty, soiled nappies into the basement. Every morning when I open my window I've got a dirty nappy looking at me. The kitchens are atrocious, absolutely filthy downstairs, so that I can't cook in that sort of conditions. I used to buy food from takeaways and things like that, but my son got ill.

He went into bed-and-breakfast when he was about four months old; he's now about fourteen months old. He's terrible: and by the time I finally do get a place of my own . . . I've got so many problems with him. Because he's not been on a proper diet, he still wakes up of a night time. he very rarely sleeps. Now he's walking, but he's still very, very small for his age. He's climbing the stairs now and twice I haven't been quick enough and he's fell down the stairs.

I've got a daughter in foster care, she'll be 16 this year and she's been in foster care now for nearly two years. It's just going from one thing to another: I'm not getting anywhere whatsoever with the councils. The hotel is not so bad, but it could be a lot better.

I can't get any social worker or health visitor – I've never had a health visitor since the baby's been born. I can't get registered with a doctor. I've lived here a year without one, and with a baby. He's been in hospital twice. He caught a virus from the hotel which was growing in his bowel. He lost over six pound in a week, he was in St Mary's Hospital for a week. Then he had a blocked intestine so he was in hospital for nearly two weeks that time.

I've never had any help from anybody whatsoever. I've done it all by myself. I went to Westminster Social Services and told them that I was so depressed I felt like going out and killing myself, and also the baby as well. And they more or less told me that they can't get involved, and if that's what I want to do, to go and do it. So the only thing that's kept me going is that I always imagine, well, I know, that there's people worse off than me. If I can help anybody else in the bed-and-breakfast then I will; and that's how I get by.

I feel so old, I mean I don't class myself as being young. I'm 34. But – I don't know – I feel so old now, so very, very old – I've just got no idea what it's going to be like when I get a place of my own. I don't even know if I'll be able to cope with housework, because I haven't had to do it.

I'll have problems with the baby when I've got a place of my own: he's always been used to being in the same room as me – eating, sleeping, playing, television. So I'll have so many problems to try and put him back in a routine, and with him having a bedroom of his own I think he's going to run riot, as well, for at least a year. Because he's never had the room, so when he does he's going to just be like a mad child.

I've got two daughters. The first one isn't with me. My first husband won custody of her. I don't know why. He's dead. He killed himself with drink and drugs, but the court awarded his common-law wife custody. She's 17 in March. My younger daughter Caroline has started playing truant from school, just so she can get to see me. She tries to get down three times a week. But being in foster care she has to be back a certain time in the evening. It would be better to have her with me, but not in bed-and-breakfast. I think we'd end up killing each other if we was in bed-and-breakfast. Even if she had her own room, it wouldn't work out. She's got so much space in her foster home. She's got her own room with all her own personal effects. They're nice people she's fostered with, very, very nice. I don't feel bad at all; in actual fact when she does finally come with me I'd like her to keep in contact with them, because they've been so good to her.

It does make me feel sad that my son's never known anything else but the hotel. But he's got a lot of years yet, so once I do get a place of my own I can make it up to him. But around here there doesn't seem to be too much to do, part from coming to Mother and Toddlers. I try to get him out every day; now he's walking he wants to walk everywhere, and he can't. It's such a busy area, main roads, I can't let him. It's too cold to go to the park, so normally we take a walk up Oxford Street, Regent Street, just looking at the shops. I try to take him to places where there's a lot of colour and a lot of lights. He's television mad at the moment, but that's all he ever sees is television.

I think there could be so much more done. I can't understand the councils; they're moaning they haven't got the money to spend on this that or the other, and yet it costs them a fortune to keep you in b-and-b. DHSS pay £48 for my room, but I think the Council makes it up to about £150 or even more now because I've moved into a bigger room. If they paid £50 a week rent, they'd save £100 just on me.

At least by the time I do get a place of my own, Adam won't have started school, so therefore I won't have to chop and change schools. But I do feel so sorry for the people that have got their kiddies in schools, and then from unforeseen circumstances they're homeless. The kiddies are put in another school and they just start to settle down, and then they're all put in a temporary let, and they start school again, and then they get in a permanent accommodation and then they've got to start school again.

I think men have it hard as well, I think they feel that they're not contributing what they should contribute to the world. But at least a man's out all day, working or whatever he's doing. Being here doesn't stop a man from doing what he wants to do. If he wants to go out and have a drink with the lads, he still goes out and has a drink with the lads. I think it makes men worse, actually, because I think they think to themselves at the end of the day, 'I've got to go back to that one bleeding room.' So they stay out, and then of course they drink a bit more. I've seen two marriages break up since I've been in the hotel.

I don't really know what could have been done to help me. You see, my husband didn't care about anything or anyone. He was good in that he got up for work every morning, very rarely had a day off. But he liked the pub as well. So I'd never get to see him. He only used to give me £46 a week to live on, and so I used to have to go to work as well. I was working all the hours God sends, just to make ends meet, but he was out having a good time. So what I was earning, he was spending. No, I've never regretted leaving him.

I should've slung him out and kept the flat myself. Instead, they've put me in bed-and-breakfast, shut the door, and now they've forgotten about me. If the Council at least had a group that came round to visit you, even once a month, to find out how you're doing and if there's somewhere they could put you where you'd find a lot more people of your own kind. They've put me into bed and breakfast where it's more or less full up with Bangladeshi families. I can't communicate to them, there's no way they can communicate to me. Don't get me wrong, I've got nothing against them. Nothing against black people. I haven't got anything against them, nothing at all. I just feel, why don't they put them in a hotel together and whites in another hotel. I suppose that's a bit selfish really, because I should imagine that would cause riots as well, with people not liking them. And then before anyone can get to like them, you have to mix with them, don't you?

When they moved me into this bigger room it was lovely. I couldn't believe it. Apart from the stairs, it was fantastic. Got my own shower, my own toilet, the room is so much bigger for Adam to play in. Then I went away for a weekend, and when I came back there was this terrible smell in the bedroom – and I knew it hadn't been me, and I knew it hadn't been Adam. I couldn't get rid of the smell. All of a sudden I heard this scratching. My brother came to visit me and he says, 'You've got pigeons, just there.' When they put the extractor fan into the shower and put the pipe right round to go on to the outside wall, they didn't block the hole up or put in any netting or anything over it. So the pigeons got in and started nesting. I went down to complain about it. And they turned round and said, 'Why should we get rid of the pigeons? Get rid of you.' So I turned round and said, 'Well that suits me fine, darling. Get rid of me, but you'll have a job getting bloody money out of the pigeons.' So that was it.

They could be a lot more helpful, if they just listened to people. But they don't care. Why should they? They're getting their money for it. They've got good homes to go to. There's four bosses in my hotel. It's two hotels in one with 36 rooms. They're all driving round in Mercedes cars, wearing smart three-piece suits. The bosses only come in maybe three times a week. For an hour. Collect the money. Go downstairs and gamble and drive off.

I don't say that they should do away with bed and breakfast altogether, but I feel that there should be a certain time in which a family should be in bed and breakfast. I think it's degrading. I think a year is more than enough. Even that is far too long. They shouldn't be selling off council houses and council flats. The Council's always turning round and saying they haven't got the properties, so why are they selling them? If a couple want to buy a home – and in this day and age good luck to anyone that can afford it – let them go and look for one. I mean why be put into a council property, and then the council sell it off? If that couple want to buy a home, they could go out and buy one and then that flat would be free again for somebody else. The whole system is bloody ridiculous. If I had any power, I'd make sure that all these empty flats were filled. Why should flats be empty for 18 months? By the time people like me move in, we've got nothing but trouble from damp and decorating and having to replace all the windows because there's been a load of kids smashing them just for the fun of it.

I've got over the stage now where I feel I'd like to commit suicide. No, you can't be like that with a small child. He's my world, my baby. I mean I think the world of my younger daughter, Caroline, but she's of an age when she can look after herself. He can't. So he's my pride and joy. Caroline's his pride and joy, and he's her pride and joy. He thinks the world of Caroline, when he sees Caroline he doesn't want Mummy any more, it's Caroline. The same with her when she comes to see us, it's kiss and cuddle for Adam, and hello Mum. But that's it. It's baby. All for baby. She's great.

When I'm rehoused, I would like to go on campaigning for homeless people. I'd like to start up a little thing by myself and just go round and visit people in bed and breakfast, just to let them know that they're not alone. Just for them to have somebody to talk to. It's terrible when you've got so much to say and there's no one there to listen.

When I first went into bed and breakfast, just after Adam was born, I was right on the very top floor. I didn't know Bayswater at all, I'd never ever been over this side. I didn't know where the shops were, I didn't have a penny to my name, I didn't know where Social Security was, I didn't know anything. I didn't even know about breakfast in the morning. I was completely lost. I think I cried from Friday to the Sunday. Especially with a hyperactive baby – he did nothing but cry anyway. I didn't make him any better, because he could sense that I was upset all the time. I didn't have anything. Nothing whatsoever. It was murderous. I didn't have a telly in my room because the previous people had stolen it. And it was only on the Wednesday that I got one. Then I started going to breakfast and I started mixing with a few people, and that was it. Now I know all the routine. Most of the people that are new come and ask me, so I can help them.

It's just my brother I see now, from before. All the friends that I did have, they all seemed to think I was wrong when I left my second husband. They didn't know the situation. They just didn't want to know any more. I can always make other friends. I just feel sorry for them: until they go through a situation like that themselves, they'll never ever know. I mean, I put up with it from my first husband. I got a bottle across the face from him. Smacked on the nose. Put in hospital when I was eight months pregnant. He was a madman. He's put a shotgun to my throat. He's tried to run me over twice. I just knew if I didn't get away properly the first time that would be it, he would kill me. He's such an evil man. He's where he belongs – six foot under.

I want to do so much! I love being married, I love doing housework, I love looking after people. I always seem to pick the wrong ones. I'd never get married again. I think it'd be disastrous. They say third time lucky, but I'm not willing to take that chance.

Me and my younger daughter couldn't stay with my second husband. My husband had been having sexual intercourse with my daughter from the age of seven until the time she went into foster care. I never knew anything about it, she never ever told me. And yet now when she sits down she talks to me – it takes her a long time. She says things . . . now, I can see it all so clearly. But why didn't I see it then? Why didn't I see it then? I couldn't. I never ever saw any of it. She might say, 'D'you remember that night you went to work and you wasn't feeling well and you come home and the door was locked?' Yes, I can now. But I didn't think anything about it at the time. And, 'Why do you think Daddy

43

wouldn't let me out on my own of an evening when you went to work? And why do you think Daddy never let me have no friends indoors? Why do you think Daddy stopped ever giving you a kiss and cuddle?' Now I can see it so clearly. Now she's nearly 16 and she's been in foster care two years now. She only told me about it because I had a row with her. I told her, 'I don't want nothing more to do with you. You're selfish.' It was only then, when I pushed her to a point where she broke down, that she told me. She said, 'Yeah, well you wouldn't like it if you'd been child abused all the time.'

I didn't know what to say. You could've knocked me over with a feather. I mean you really could. Me and my husband used to sit down and, 'Yes,' I used to say, 'I'd love to catch one. By God I'd put him in a room full of mothers.' And he used to say, 'Yeah, dirty swines.' He was doing it himself.

I would never have thought that of him, because he brought her up since she was 18 months. She told me last year, she told me round about June. Her foster parents know and her social worker knows. I was the last to know. Because she was frightened to tell me in case I called her a liar. But no, I never called her a liar.

It happened to me when I was a child. So I know exactly what she's gone through. I mean my brother used to do it to me, my brother used to hold a knife at my throat and say if I ever, ever told anybody, I'd be put in prison. The only time I ever spoke about it was when Caroline told me about her. And then I told her I'd been through it. . . But why? I mean I never ever denied him anything. If he wanted to make love, that was fine by me. I've never ever turned him away. He's always had everything he's ever wanted. Whether I felt like it or whether I didn't. I was there: just for that reason, that if I say no to him, he's going to go and get it somewhere else. But the last three years of us being together, he never ever touched me. I just thought it was because of his drinking.

Still, that's another problem we've got over. We will get over it. Life still goes on. You'll never forget, you never ever forgive the person, but at least it seems to be easier to live with. At the time you feel dirty and you never ever want to go with another man – but time is a great healer. I will get her over it. She knows now that she can talk to me about anything that she wants to, because I've been through it and there's nothing now that can shock me, about what men do to women. Nothing at all. But it's very hard. At the same time, I try not to tar every man with the same brush. But it's so hard, because I've found two bad ones.

I'll get over it. She'll get over it. And we'll make the best of what we've got. I'll make sure that, while she's with me, she'll never have to suffer any of them things any more. It's made her more aware of men. When she's got children of her own, at least she'll know. Because it's happened to her. She'll spot the signs – that I didn't spot! I always thought I would, but I didn't. I said to her, if she wants a job, do it while the children are at school. Don't do it while they're at home. Don't ever work then. Because that's what I done. I worked so hard. And I worked hard to let her have the things that I never had.

A year after this interview, I was unable to trace Angela. I heard from a reliable source that she had accepted an offer of a flat on a council estate in South-East London.

Doris

Doris came from Jamaica as a child, and has lived in London since she was 12. As a single woman with no children, she would not normally have qualified for rehousing under the Homeless Persons' Act. She did so because an emergency, in this case a fire in her private sector flat, made her homeless. Doris used to do temporary office jobs. When I interviewed her she was doing a City Lit. Breakthrough course as well as working as a volunteer for MIND, and for the Bayswater Project. She would like to do an Open University course in psychology.

Doris is 41, with an expressive face and voice. She cried when she was describing the fire that made her homeless and again, with laughter, when she was telling me about the flat she turned down. She is strong and articulate, which undoubtedly made it easier for her to fight her way out of bed and breakfast. After six months she was permanently rehoused, in the attractive top floor Servite flat overlooking Westminster Cathedral where I interviewed her. This interview shows that persistent protest *can* work.

I was burnt out of my flat on the seventh of June 1986, about one-twenty in the morning. I was asleep and you know how you hear a distant sound? The smoke detector had gone off before but I thought, I might as well go out and have a look. I went out in the hall and it was full of smoke and people running up and down the stairs. I ran down the stairs and there was fire and flames pouring out of the building. There was two little fires in the hallway; someone got the fire extinguisher and put them out. Then I ran back upstairs and knocked on the door of the girl next door, because she had a baby. She'd realised and was coming out. Half-way down the stairs, the lights went off. We got out, went across the road and waited.

I didn't even have shoes. I had a tracksuit on and a T-shirt that I used to sleep in. On the first floor the fire wasn't too bad, on my side. The roof of all three buildings collapsed, one house was completely demolished, the concrete stairs collapsed. There were people in the third building who couldn't get out. Two people died. It was awful to watch the people who couldn't get down, because the fire was so fierce. The fire engine hadn't arrived. There wasn't a ladder to get one of the blokes down, and he was screaming. I can still hear him.

Some of us were taken away in a police van about five in the morning. We went into the hotel across the road and they made us all tea and gave us all blankets. Then we were taken to a D H S S place. Someone said that because we were all single they couldn't help us, which they later denied. But at the time I didn't realise that, because we were burnt out, the Council had a duty to rehouse us.

When I went back, about ten the next morning, Helen from the Bayswater Project was outside the building. She came downstairs to the basement when I was sitting there. We didn't know what we were going to do; there was no electricity in the building and nobody knew what was happening. We were all still suffering from shock, really. And Helen said that the Council had a duty to rehouse us, and we told her what they'd said and she said that was rubbish, and we should all go down the Homeless Unit in Crawford Place. I didn't even know that such a thing existed.

So she took four of us in a taxi and they booked us into the Eden Park Hotel. I've got family in London, but they didn't have room to put me up. It would have been a bit awkward, so it seemed that the only reasonable alternative was to go to a hotel, because somehow I imagined it was going to be a short thing. I didn't for one minute think I was going to be there more than the weekend, you know? I just couldn't contemplate staying there seven months. It didn't seem real, somehow.

I was lucky in a way that I had a friend who lived not far away, so I was able to use her flat; she gave me the key. She used to make sure I was eating. You know, you don't feel like eating, you don't feel like doing anything, because the psychological effect of it is quite devastating. You just feel you want to sit down and cry all the time. She was also very supportive – which is something a lot of people don't have. Because when you're in a situation like that, you feel so vulnerable. You tend to stay away from people because you feel so angry, you feel so guilty about what's happened, because somehow in society it's almost as if it's your fault. In English society, when things happen, it's your fault, and you're not supposed to show any emotion, you're supposed to pull yourself together and get on with it. So I did try and stay away from people – even from my family.

I did tell my family, but not most of my friends. They kept ringing round each other, trying to find out what had happened. It's – so difficult to explain, because unless you've actually experienced it yourself – I mean it's a year and eight months since it happened, and still I have to fight back the tears, talking about it; it's still so traumatic. It's fading but it's still sore, it's like having a scar that's not red raw anymore but it's still painful, you know?

While I was in the hotel I got involved with forming the Committee at the Bayswater Project. I thought that was the only way we could fight the Council, because they were bullshitting us a lot. Westminster would ring up people and tell them they had to move out of their hotel one minute, then the next they'd go there and deny they ever said it. They wouldn't put anything in writing. The Homeless Unit said they didn't agree with it, but they had to comply even though they thought it was wrong because if they didn't they would lose their job, and good luck if we wanted to fight the Council. So we formed the Committee, with Helen's help, and I was very active, organising meetings, writing to MPs, going up to Victoria Street to talk to the Deputy Director of Housing – I got a lot of my anger out that way. Although there were times when I was depressed and I felt really low, because every time you tried something – I could sit there and write to about fifty housing trusts, send off letters, and make telephone calls, send off application forms – and they'd all come back with the same thing: 'No, no, we can't accept you, you have to be nominated by the Council.' And the Council were saying, 'No, we won't nominate you, because you're single and able-bodied.'

Westminster Council had a meeting and they decided to prioritise things. They created the crisis themselves; they all get in a mess, as a direct result of Government policy. There's vast amounts of homelessness; local authorities haven't got the funding because the Government have cut it, they're selling off houses, whereas in the past they used to be able to borrow money and use the rates to pay that money back, the Government have stopped them doing it. So because they don't know what to do, they say only people with a medical problem or over 50 can get a flat.

I was working while I was in the hotel. Then I got caught in the Social Security trap, because the hotel cost so much – £35 a night. It was a grubby little room. You had a single bed, the springs had gone in it. I'm still going to the osteopath for my back. There's about a foot of space to stand in, and a wardrobe and a toilet. Oh God, it was so depressing, because it was at the back, it didn't overlook anything. All the restaurants of Queensway, all the smells coming in. And the noise, they're up until one in the morning . . . About three months after I got into the hotel I had to stop work because the DHSS wanted to charge me. Because I was working, they would only give me £30 of my salary.

Say, for example, I was temping, if I earned £150 that week they would give me £30, and keep the rest. Because with temping, some weeks you work, some weeks you don't, it does cause quite a lot of hassle. The thing was, that if I wasn't working, I'd end up with £35 or £36 a week. You can't work, because if you work you're caught in this trap.

I just used to go to bed at night, get up in the morning and get out, to survive. I just couldn't stay there. I didn't make friends in the hotel. I suppose I didn't really want to make friends. Maybe it's snobbish but you don't choose your neighbours, and if you had to choose them, you wouldn't live next door to them! I'd rather choose my own friends. You choose your friends because people have got an interest in the same things or because you read the same books. I didn't really find the atmosphere in the hotel menacing because I didn't notice it much. A lot of people did. People with families would, because of the way the managers treat them.

I'm not English, I was born in Jamaica and came here when I was 12. So my cultural upbringing until I was 12 is a greater influence.

I don't think it's wrong to get angry: I just *get* angry. People there found that very threatening, because I used to just stand there and shout at them. I didn't just sit and take it. Once there was no heating, I just went downstairs and asked the manager for a heater. He said, 'We haven't got any.' I said, 'I'll just wait until you get one.' So I just stood there and waited, and he went and got me one.

There's this thing in England that you don't confront things, or you don't confront people, you just sit and take it. In a way, that's why this government gets away with what it does. Because there's no confrontation, people don't know how to fight. There's this suppression of all your emotions, you're not supposed to get mad: you *should* get mad as hell if something upsets you. It's *very* unhealthy not to. You can imagine if this government was in Italy, they'd most probably go and shoot Mrs Thatcher. There'd be rioting in the streets. It's amazing that people in England are not aware of their emotions. There's so much suppression of your feelings.

In the hotel where I was some people were saying they were frightened to complain. They had been told that if they complained any more than they were going to be thrown out. The minute they were threatened they all came running to me. I'd ring Helen or the solicitor, and he'd get on to them, and it'd stop. The Council wrote me a letter telling me to come down; I never went. I thought, You can bugger off. I'm not going chasing after you. So I wasn't treated the same way as everyone else, because when I went down there I always stuck up for myself. And whatever they told me, I'd say, 'Well, you put it in writing.'

They'd always back down. You have to be aggressive. The thing is, people in England are frightened of being shouted at. The only way is to be – not aggressive, but assertive; there is a difference. To stand up for yourself in a very positive and demanding way without being rude. And that's what I did. I'd say, 'Do you think, because I'm homeless, that I'm any less a human being than anyone else?'

I think being homeless sharpened my perceptions. I was always aware of certain things, but not to the same extent; it really opened my eyes. When you're comfortable, you've got a job and holidays and you can do things, you're having a fairly normal life – you don't think of the underdogs. You see it and you think, People create (poverty) for themselves; that's what the media give out. I thought it was only those sort of people who were homeless. It didn't apply to me. That's one of the shocks when it does happen to you, because of the stigma that's attached to it. Then you change your attitude to homelessness. On the other hand you don't want to sit around and brood about it all the time, because it's depressing. Now, having a flat, feeling comfortable again, I don't want to start thinking about being homeless. You have to detach yourself from it because psychologically it's the only way you can survive. I can understand why people don't want to think about it: it threatens their security. They would feel very vulnerable if they sat and thought, well, this could happen to me. It would scare the shit out of you. So people don't think about it. It has to be something that happens to other people.

It's a big problem. I don't really know how we can draw more attention to it – I suppose by campaigning and showing that homeless people are normal. If you're articulate and you can get on the box and talk . . . Lyn and Claire, from the Project, are really articulate and they can express their anger, express themselves in a positive way. It's a gift; there are a lot of people not capable of being like that, who can't stand up and be counted. That's the sort of problem they've had all their lives; it's got nothing to do with being homeless.

It does happen to women a lot, I think partly because women are not meant to express anger. They turn it inwards and they become depressed. The women in the hotels were frightened that if they got angry they'd take it out on their children. Women don't want to batter their children; it's just the anger they're feeling at the time. It might not belong to the situation that's happening, it might be about something that happened three or four years ago – it's like the straw that breaks the camel's back. The *stress*!

It was difficult to accept being homeless. I mean even the *word* is just so awful. God, my stomach used to go into an absolute knot. Then there's the shock of realising, This is going to take longer than I thought. It was then that I really started to fight and get angry.

My doctor was absolutely wonderful. If it wasn't for her, I would not have got this place. I had another doctor before, for 20 years. He was absolutely useless. The day of the fire I went round to see him. I was in tears, and he was talking to me and writing at the same time. He wouldn't even look at me. It was just awful. I was SO angry. He gave me a prescription for Valium, and said, 'I can't do anything else.' So I just went out into the street and I tore the prescription to shreds. It was my friend who said, 'Why don't you go to my doctor? She's very good, very considerate and caring.' In the end I went to her and she took me on. She was marvellous! She said, 'What you need is a place to live. I'm not going to give you any tablets because you don't need them.' She said, 'Right, we'll do a letter. Take it up to the Housing Office in the Harrow Road.' She let me read it. She said there were medical reasons why the Council had to rehouse me. About two weeks after she sent the letter I got one from them, asking me to fill in another form. I thought, Jesus, more bloody filling in forms. I rang the bloke in the Housing Office up, and said, 'What do you want to know my address for? You've got my address, you've sent me the form, it's here!' So he said, 'People like you it takes longer.'

Three days after that I had a letter asking me to go down there to view a flat down by Pimlico Barracks, by the dustbins if you please! Bloody dustcarts going up the back! It's a dump! I took the key and I was all excited – I walked in, I couldn't believe it. The place smelt awful – I looked out the back and there were all these bloody dustcarts whizzing up and down. And the noise! There was a sort of makeshift double glazing, and it was right on top of the depot where they keep all the dustcarts, going out at five or six in the morning. In the kitchen, there was this stove, like something out of Noah's ark! I was furious! The woman from the Council said to me, 'Are you taking the flat?' I said, 'You're joking, it's a fucking dump!' She said, 'It's not as bad as that.' I said, 'Well, if you don't think it's as bad as that you go and live in it.' I walked off. I thought, that's it, I'm not going to hear from them again. I walked nearly all the way to Bayswater, I was in such a temper.

About a week after that, there was a letter from this Housing Trust, the Servites. They came on the Friday, and the next Tuesday, I got a letter to say I'd got it. I moved in December. It's £30, about £40 with rates.

All the solutions to homelessness cost money. An ideal situation to me would be to have a group session for all the mothers – or fathers – who are in b-and-b which they can go to once a week, and talk about what they're feeling. A group that's chaired by a proper therapist, who's going to sit there and allow them to act out all the feelings that they're suppressing, to express all the anger and to make them aware that it's perfectly normal to be angry. People don't believe it is, and they feel guilty about it. If you can make them feel it's okay to have those feelings, then they'll get up and start fighting! All that costs money. In English society, everything boils down to that. Can't service the trains properly, because it costs too much money. Never mind if you all burn to death on the Underground. We won't have proper sprinklers because it costs too much money. It's just crazy! Everybody's in a state of apathy. Nobody gives a damn! Everybody's lost their will to fight. It's pathetic, it really is, everybody just accepts their lot.

How can you have a government with no backbenchers to oppose? They don't oppose nothing. Like a bunch of wallies! They haven't got an ounce of backbone between them, they're like lambs to the slaughter. She just tells them all what to do and they just run and do it. We had a lecture on Freud where the lecturer said that men were frightened of women. I have never seen such a classic case of what Freud's talking about – all those men are terrified of Mrs Thatcher. What we do need is a strong Labour woman leader to oppose her in Parliament.

Ginny

Ginny is 28, with fair hair and blue eyes, a heavy smoker. Her voice was exhausted and numb. I first met her when she came with her younger son to the toy library. She, her husband and their four children were living in one room in a hotel next door.

I decided to interview Ginny because her story shows how quickly a string of misfortunes can lead to homelessness. In her case, repossession of a house and sexual assault drove her to a breakdown. The hotel room she and her family lived in was, at £714 a week, one of the most expensive I heard of. Ginny's husband has worked whenever he could but frequent moves have made this difficult. As she says, jobs are in London but they couldn't get housing there.

The 'intentionally homeless' clause in the Housing Act (1985) is one of the ways in which local authorities weed out people who have passed the first two tests to establish that they are 'priority homeless'. As Mary Tester's interview makes clear, shortage of housing makes it necessary to define more and more people as 'intentionally homeless'. This means the local authority can decide that a woman is responsible for her own homelessness, and that it has no responsibility to house her even though she may have young children. The 'intentionally homeless' are people whose intentions and needs are considered irrelevant. For Ginny and her family, having a pet, never mind a home, was an impossible luxury.

I've got four children, aged seven, five, four and nearly two. We owned property in Bournemouth and we had to sell it because it was going to be repossessed. We ended up with £2,000 so we went to Manchester and got a deposit on a house down there. When we'd been there a few weeks my little girl was sexually assaulted by the boy that lived next door. I got the police, she was examined and they could see she'd been interfered with but there wasn't anything they could do because they said there wasn't enough evidence. I ended up having a nervous breakdown. I was in a psychiatric hospital for three weeks. When I came out I went right back to the state I was in before. This boy kept getting

53

her over the fence: there was nothing I could do to keep him away from her. He was fifteen and she was six. The social worker down there said to my husband, 'If you want your wife to stay sane and to keep your daughter safe, the only thing I can say is leave.' We gave the keys back to the Building Society. That's how we became homeless.

We're not stupid people, to turn round and give up a house we were buying to end up living in a caravanette. We've got one and we lived in that for a few weeks. We've really tried hard to get our own private accommodation. The cheapest house we could find was £130 a week. Doing that, my husband would have to stay on Social all the time because there's no way he could get a job and afford that rent. Most private houses won't take children anyway.

We came down to Brent Council because we used to live in Brent. After six months in a bed-and-breakfast hotel, they have found us intentionally homeless, so they want us to leave. We'll go and live with my father-in-law; it's the only option left to us now. He's got a two-bedroom flat ten floors up, so it's not ideal but it's better than one room with four children.

Bed and breakfast isn't an ideal situation for families. We're six flights up, with just a small room. Four beds, bathroom facilities are two flights down, the kitchen is seven flights down. It's very dirty, I don't use it if I can help it. There's 55 rooms in the hotel and the average is three to a room, so you can imagine the amount of people that are using the kitchens. There are four bathrooms. Most of the rooms have got showers. If you can get the bath, or get a plug for it, then a clean bath is all right. But trying to get children under a shower just doesn't work, they just won't get under it. I'm lucky, I go to my father-in-law's in Essex at weekends and bath the children over there.

My room costs £714 a week. It's called bed and breakfast. You get a stale roll, a hard-boiled egg and a pat of butter in a carrier bag and that's your breakfast. You take it up to your room. The dangers – I mean the stairs, the carpets have come undone. My little boy's slipped down twice, I've gone flying once with my little baby in my arms. The amount of times we've put in complaints that it should be fixed, and they just don't do it. You're living in squalor. They're paying that amount of money for you to live in squalor.

All the owners of the hotels want is the money. They don't care how you're treated. The place is crawling with cockroaches, silverfish, it's just completely dirty. It's gone right back to the Stone Age. Homeless people are just treated as nobodies. The amount of money it's costing the government, you'd think they'd do something about it. The only thing that's wrong with homeless people is, they need a home. They're not the scum of the earth, they're not villains, they've done nothing wrong.

We never told them about the house in Manchester. I didn't want it all to come out, what happened to my daughter. They found out about it and, to punish us, they said they was moving us from this hotel, because it was too expensive, to another. We got to the other hotel and there was a room eight by twelve with a double bed and a single bed, and that was it for the six of us. Luckily Shelagh O'Brien, who runs the Bayswater Project, managed to get in touch with the emergency Council man, and he said we'd have to go back to Margaret Brook House. When we got back to the hotel, our room had gone already, and we had to go six flights up – before, we were on the ground floor. When the Bayswater Project got in touch with Brent Council to find out what was happening, they said the official reason was Brent couldn't afford it, but the unofficial reason was we were being punished for not telling them about the house.

I thought it was all wrong. Fair enough, punish me and my husband, fine us if they had to, but not the children as well. We came back to this hotel and then the Bayswater Project said there was going to be an appeal. The appeal went against us so now Brent have asked us to leave bed-and-breakfast, go and live with my father-in-law like I said. They said we might still get an offer, but it will be outside of London not in Brent. But until you've got it in writing you can't believe what the Council says. Unless I've got it in black and white I'll be very reluctant to leave the hotel. They'll have to take me to court. My husband could have got work here. But you're just not stable, it's here today gone tomorrow. The Council can do what they like with you. They phoned us up to say we were moving. It was quarter past four, Friday night, and they told us we had to be out of the hotel nine o'clock Saturday morning. So if my husband was out at work, there's no way we could do it. My husband said, 'I want to go and look at the place first. If it's worse than what I'm living in then I don't want to move into it.' And the Council said to him, 'You go where we tell you, you've got no choice.' I was over at my father-in-law's, I was ill, so he took me over there for a bit of rest. The Council wanted my phone number. They wanted to get through to my father-in-law to tell me to start packing because we were moving the next day. They run your life, you've no privacy. They want to know where you are, what you're doing, every minute of the day. It's worse than being in prison. You've just no freedom.

My husband went for an interview over the weekend and he's got a job to start after Christmas. With a stable address at my father-in-law's, he's in full-time work. So it just goes to show. He could have got a job at any time, but I couldn't stand the pressure in the hotel on my own and we couldn't take the risk of being moved at a moment's notice. It's working out well for us, except that we're going to be overcrowded. But it can't be more overcrowded than one room.

Six weeks later I went to see Ginny in her father-in-law's tenth-floor flat in Essex. She met me at the station with her father-in-law, a heavy man in his sixties with a vast, booming voice (he is a retired toastmaster). He drove us to a tower block on a hill, wreathed in fog, and left us to talk in the living room. Ginny seemed even more tense than before. She chain-smoked and talked about the crash diet she was on. Opposite the couch where we sat was an array of bottles of spirits, upside-down, ready to be poured. Ginny told me that she had been drinking three-quarters of a bottle of Bacardi a day. On the sideboard were photographs of Ginny and her father-in-law, dressed up, at some function. Her little boy played in the room while we talked. I asked whether she was glad that they had moved there instead of staying in bed and breakfast.

Well, I know I should turn around and say I am, but no, I'm not. I'd much rather have stayed in the bed and breakfast than have moved up here with my father-in-law. It's a two-bedroomed flat, it's ten floors up, and it is so dangerous. We've been here for three weeks, and Monday, for the first time, I opened the windows to get rid of the condensation, because it's very bad up here. I've had a cat for five years and I brought her up to Dad's with us. A friend had been looking after her while I was in b-and-b. I was in the kitchen when I heard Bobby screaming and shouting, so I went into the bedroom and he was up on the windowsill. If I'd've gone two seconds later he'd've been out of the window.

And what I didn't realise, but found out a few hours later, was that my cat had gone. She fell out of the window and broke her neck. Now two seconds later, that could have been Robert down. My father-in-law, he's lived here for years, and trying to get him to close windows – we've put locks on the windows but if I go out of the flat for anything, I find all the locks undone, all the windows open. I have to go round closing them all up again, and it's causing a bit of friction, because he wants them open. He just doesn't realise the danger, no matter how much I say to him. It's played a lot more on my nerves now, living up here.

I've tried to get in touch with Brent to find out when I'm going to get housed. I could be up here for a year. It just isn't going to work. I can see my father-in-law getting so uptight, telling us to go in the end. And then where do we go? Brent Council said we could only stay in bed-and-breakfast until March, but they would rather we moved up here sooner to save them some money, which we did, over Christmas. But now, talking to Brent, they're talking about another five or six months. Yet if we'd've been in bed and breakfast we'd've got an offer by March. It's as if they're saying, 'Well, they've got a roof over their heads now, forget them.' Which just isn't fair. Not this high up, anyway. I mean I went to the doctor's yesterday – my nerves are just absolutely ended. I told him everything that'd happened from the time we sold our house in Bournemouth. He said, 'I'm not surprised you're depressed. I would be if I'd gone through what you've gone through. It's not tablets you need, it's a change of circumstances.' He gave me some tablets, to try to relax, but that's all he said he could do. It's dreadful the way people are treated, I just can't understand it.

I think we could afford a mortgage, now my husband's working, but we won't be given one, because we walked away from the house in Manchester. We gave that back to the Building Society. We didn't sell it, we just gave the keys back and stopped paying and they repossessed it. I don't think we'd get another mortgage, unless my husband did a bit of ducking and diving, which he's good at. The job he's on now, his wages were £215, he brought home £150. But he's written off for another job now, for Continental driving, a week in Italy and a week in the UK. That sort of job is paying nearly £300 a week. So we could afford a mortgage, if we can get around to it. I think if he does get the job, and he's steady, that's what we'll have to end up doing.

The work's in London, for my husband, so we would rather stay here, but to buy outside of London – I mean there's just no work. So, he's got the work in London but we haven't got any house. If he could earn the wages elsewhere that he's earning here, you know, we'd be laughing for a place, somewhere cheap. But I can't see it ever happening. Prices are just too high. It's all right saying it's an investment, but how on earth do you get the mortgage repayments? I don't understand people these days that are buying a one-bedroom flat for £65,000. How on earth do they pay the mortgage?

The place we bought in Bournemouth was really a beautiful, big house. Our mortgage repayments were nearly £300 a month, and we were struggling with that. I started to take in people for b-and-b. I enjoyed it, it was good, I got on well with the people. I had four rooms which I let, either to couples or singles or two girls, two boys sharing. It was mainly couples with children that I let to. Because it was only four rooms that I let, we got on really well. I let the people use the back garden for the children, or if ever I could hear the mums getting uptight, screaming at the children, I'd always say, 'Do you want me to take him for a while? D'you want to go and do some shopping?' or I'd say, 'D'you want to come down and sit with me? I'm sat on my own doing nothing.' And we'd just sit down and chat.

So the pressures weren't there like they are where I was in bed and breakfast. I think it's because it's done on such a large scale. It's so impersonal. When I was in Margaret Brook House nobody spoke to each other. There were about 58 rooms. It's almost as if everyone was trying to keep their own rooms, their own privacy, and you just ignored each other. Never got involved with anybody, never spoke to anybody. It's unbelievable. My two children played with two Indian children, they made a good little friendship between them, and we made friends with the parents that way. But there was a lot of children and you never saw them. The mothers either kept them in the room or they went out for the day, and just came back at night time. A lot of the parents would let the children play out in the hallways. You'd stop to say hello to a child and they'd look at you as if you were funny as if to say, Who are you saying hello to? It is sad, because I mean you're all in the same boat. I think it is the way the hotel was run.

You had to walk in, sign on, sign out, it was worse than being at Colditz, you know. Everybody felt like that. They didn't have a television room, nothing. You used to be able to go down to the kitchen to do your cooking. There was about five stoves down there – which isn't a lot for over a hundred people to share. It was so mixed. You had Indians, coloured people, Iranians – I think there was about three English families there. You'd have thought we would have clung together, but we didn't. You'd go down into the kitchen and hear all this foreign language going on so you never felt comfortable anyway. Just felt like you was in a different bloody country.

Yet I would much prefer to be back in the room, because I felt safer. Being so high up and having that shock over the baby – it's frightened the life out of me. I can't send the children down, let them play out the front. They can't reach the button to get back up to the tenth floor. Candy can just jump up and press the lift button for it to open and close, but she can't reach the tenth.

The good thing about the flats is the playroom on every floor. You see, although they're council flats, they weren't originally built as council flats, they were built privately, to be sold. But the money ran out, so council took them over. You don't see any toys in here because they're all out in the playroom. But up above the sixth floor there aren't any children, because that's council policy, apparently. Whether Havering Council know we're here, I don't know. I'm worried that if I let them know that we're here, they might turn round and say get out. Then where do I go?

What do I think could be done to make all this better? I'd get rid of the b-and-b for a start. I would get in touch with landlords, about letting places for temporary accommodation. No sitting tenants. Say they gave a family like mine a house which cost a £120 a week. Then, with the other £600 they were saving, not putting me in one room in Bayswater, they could start to build more houses. It's getting to the stage where they're offering people accommodation which is really unfit for humans to live in. But they're taking it just because it's their own place. I can't understand how it's got in such a bad way, anyway. All these homeless families, it's unbelievable.

It's almost as if the country's telling you now that wherever you're living, no matter what happens, if you leave that place it's somehow your fault. You've no choice where you want to live these days. You just can't move round the country any more.

At the moment, here, the girl and the two boys are in with their grandad and the baby's in the bedroom with us. So the grandad doesn't get much sleep. At weekends they're up at the crack of dawn or getting up for school during the week. I mean he goes out working some nights – he's retired but he has a little job behind a bar. He might not get in until eleven or twelve. Once or twice he's come shouting at me and my husband: 'Sort your kids out, I've had enough of them.' You can understand the pressure on him as well. It used to be just him and Mum up here, they were so used to the quietness I suppose, it's a big change for him as well. We got on much better when we was in the b-and-b place. We all got on great. But actually living with each other, it just doesn't work, no matter how you love each other.

I'm not a very good person for putting up with pressure anyway. The other day my husband says to me, 'What's the matter, luv? You've not been too clever these last few days. What's wrong?' I says, 'Nothing that jumping out of the window wouldn't solve.'

I said to my husband, 'I don't care where it is, even if I have to end up putting bars on the bloody windows, padlocks on the doors, wherever we get housed we're going to stay.'

When my daughter was first born we went into b-and-b, and it broke my marriage up for a while. So when we left Bournemouth I was determined not to go back. Even when we left the place in Manchester we tried everything. We just couldn't do it. It was getting near winter, there was no heating in the caravanette. So we had to go up to the Council. We sat down and we agreed that, no matter how bad the pressures got, we would try and talk it out with each other instead of ending up splitting up like we did last time. Fingers crossed, we did it quite well.

It's nice for the children here. They're not sort of blocked into one room all the time. I notice more difference with the baby because he can get around a lot better. The fact that they've got their own beds – they had them in the b-and-b place but it was Mum and Dad in the same room, the telly on and the kettle boiling. They've actually got a kichen where they can sit down and eat their meals – the children are definitely a lot happier. I am as well, to be able to have my own kitchen, to go out and prepare the children's tea, and then get my father-in-law's and my husband's tea ready – that takes a lot of the pressure off. I think if Dad was on the second floor, I wouldn't be under this pressure. It's just the height that frightens me, specially after losing the cat. We'd been up here three weeks and she sat up at the windows a lot, and even when they were open just a little bit to let air in she was never bothered. I blame myself. I keep thinking, if I left her with Mary in London she'd still be alive now. I would never get another one like her, so it wouldn't be worth it. I couldn't love another cat the way I loved her. I might get a budgie for the children or something.

In February 1989 I talked to Ginny again. After months of sexual harassment from her father-in-law, she had walked out on him and also split up from her husband. She then spent two months in a battered wives' refuge with her four children. It was only because she was considered particularly vulnerable that she was, in April 1988, given a permanent three-bedroomed flat in Harrow Hill. When I spoke to her she had just had another baby.

Months after they left her father-in-law's flat, Ginny's eight-year-old daughter told her that her grandfather had sexually assaulted her. Ginny told me that he had just been arrested.

60

Helen

Helen and her husband, who are both 25, belong to a generation of Irish people who can't find work in their own country. They have two small sons, Bernard and Douglas. Helen worked as a medical secretary until her elder son was born and her husband was working as an industrial driver in North London.

According to the Irish Embassy, unemployment in Southern Ireland stands at 19.5 per cent, and is slightly higher in Northern Ireland. An estimated 26,000–30,000 people a year, most of them young and qualified, have left Southern Ireland since 1982. About 70 per cent of them are thought to come to England. These statistics are not reliable because there are, of course, no immigration controls between England and Ireland, although Patricia Kirwan says in a later interview she would like to impose them.

Under the 1986 Housing and Planning Act, a council sending a family back to Ireland must establish that an Irish authority has an empty property with 'minimum standard' to offer that family. On 13 November 1987, Labour-controlled Camden repatriated several Irish families against their will, saying that their policy was brought about by a chronic lack of resources and was not racist. Two months earlier, the Council began giving travel warrants back to Ireland to families who they decided were 'intentionally homeless'. A report by the Association of Metropolitan Authorities, published on 19 April 1988, said that Camden had the same duty to secure accommodation for applicants with no local connections as for those with connections, and that the offer of travel warrants to unintentionally homeless families 'risked racial discrimination'.

My husband and I lived here for five years. Then we went back to Ireland, but the job prospects didn't work out. He was working when we went back first, then he was unemployed there for ten months and it was unbearable. So we came back here, and he was no sooner back here than he got work again. When we came back to look for accommodation, we got offered a lot of places but once we mentioned that we had children, they didn't want us. Douglas is three and a half and Bernard is two. We were refused on so many occasions by landlords once they knew we had children, we'd no other alternative but to turn to the housing unit. They placed us in bed and breakfast, and we're there now for almost four months.

When we first went into b-and-b it was strange, because I suppose I'd always lived in a home environment, in a house or a flat, and it was so different, you know, having no table, having no couch, just beds to sit on, beds to eat on, beds to entertain on. I thought I'd never really adjust to it, but one has to.

In the beginning I used to go down to breakfast in the morning, but it wasn't practical, really, because the children used never to eat down there. There was always other children running round, and they used to want to run around with them, and it was such a waste of food anyway. They never ate what was put in front of them. And there was always men there, looking at them. So I usually give the children cereal in the room and have a cup of tea. You see the kitchen doesn't open until half eleven – so you have to wait until then before you can have a slice of toast or a bacon sandwich or something. Which is bad, really – specially on Sunday. Well, every day is bad, really.

I'm lucky, because I've got a husband. A lot of the women in the hotel are single or they're separated, and they have to take their children down to the kitchen with them. I never cook until my husband gets home, no matter what time it is – he usually gets home about half seven – so that they can stay in the room with him. Because the kitchen is a hazardous area; there's all these work tops and saucepans and pots, and there's about 11 ovens all on together and they can easily get burned and scalded.

There's 407 rooms in the hotel. I don't really know how much they pay for us but I'm sure it's well over £500 a week, because we have two rooms, separated by steps. We have our own bathroom and toilet, which is quite good really. It's between £500 and £700 a week at least, which is a complete and utter waste of money. I'm sure we'd get rented accommodation – a two-bedroom house anywhere – for £120 a week.

Douglas keeps saying, 'How come, Mummy, they have a table and we don't have a table, how come they've got a couch and we haven't got a couch?' He realises the difference between a house and a room like we're in. It is sad, really. All his other friends at three and a half are at nursery and they do various things. He just comes to the Bayswater Centre here, but it's not the same because I stay here and he can run to me all the time. He does ask questions and sometimes it's difficult to answer them, too. I don't tell them we're in a hotel, I always try to convince them it's a house.

I wouldn't consider going back to Ireland. I think it's better to be employed here than unemployed in Ireland. It's not good for a marriage for a person to be unemployed – for my marriage, anyway. When my husband was unemployed it was really hell. He'd nothing to do every day, he used to get up about ten or twelve and then he'd nothing to do with himself for the rest of the day. It used to grate on me when I'd see him sitting round the house doing nothing. Once he'd go out, I'd stay in, and once he'd come in, I'd go out, because we couldn't stay in the house together; we were always arguing and bickering. Since we came back this has never happened; we get on famously, really. Except that we haven't got a house.

If you want to survive you have to cope, you have to have patience, you have to put the children first. I think, since I came into the bed-and-breakfast, I tend to lose my patience a lot more. Little things get to me: they spill something on the carpet! That really annoys me, because you can see all the stains, things like that.

In our hotel people do make friends. In the kitchen we're always talking to one another and there's all different people from different nationalities, and we're all cooking something different. You learn how to make curries and cook different sorts of food, which is good. Lots of women in the hotel are very nice. There are some men I don't like. There's one man in particular: he's always teasing my two boys and putting them crying. I think he hasn't got any children of his own and he's always trying to make trouble for these two, you know? Being mean to them and saying they're doing something they're not actually doing. He's quite young, in his thirties. We don't really help each other with the children, in the hotel. I think a lot of people have been there longer than I, they've kind of accumulated their own friends. I've got my friends from the Bayswater Centre, so that's why I don't go about with them. I know the ones in the kitchen and that's it, you know?

I've told some of them about the Bayswater Centre but a lot of mothers don't want to come and sit here. I think it's fantastic, it's good for the children and it's good for me. The same people come every day and we're all homeless as well.

When we were in Ireland and we thought of coming back to England I had no idea what it would be like. I didn't think we'd have such difficulty, really, in finding a place. When I was pregnant with Douglas I found accommodation just like that, and my landlord knew. Actually we were hoping to get another flat from him, but nothing came up, because the people that have his flats don't leave him, unless it's to buy properties. None of the other landlords wanted us. I think it's getting stricter now. People don't want the children. So much has changed, really, which is depressing. I did hear about bed and breakfast. But I think I never took any notice of it until I actually became homeless myself. I often remember seeing films on television and things like that, but when you're not in the circumstances, I don't think it sinks in as much, really. I know what it is now and I think I'd be willing to talk about it more and share my views. People that haven't experienced it don't know.

I have just received a letter saying that I made myself intentionally homeless. We're very insecure because we don't know from one day to the next what's happening. We could be moved to any part of London, and with my husband working, I don't really know what's going to happen. He has to go to Cricklewood every morning to pick some people up, to take to work, so if he's sent miles away I don't know what he's going to do. He'll just have to stop his work and become unemployed. I wouldn't like that. He drives machinery. He's working full-time now; he always has, except when he was unemployed in Ireland.

Rents have gone up so much we couldn't afford to pay unless we were both working full-time, definitely not, and with rates, gas bills, electric bills and everything, we couldn't afford it, no way.

The Council are saying people are intentionally homeless because they don't want to house you, they don't want to be responsible. But what really maddens me, is that so many flats and houses are now vacant! I know of quite a few. When there's somebody working that would be willing to pay for one, too: I can never understand to this day why they let the flats stay vacant. My husband, he's quite a handyman, and would do the flat up and everything himself, which wouldn't cost the Council anything. But they're not interested in saving money. It doesn't make sense, certainly not. For example, there are four of us and none of us goes for breakfast: obviously we should be able to tell the Council that and it should be deducted. There are a lot of other people that don't go for breakfast. It's not the food, it's because the atmosphere isn't nice. Take the heating – the hotel is so hot! The corridors, the kitchen, every place. It's unbearably hot. They're spending thousands – hundreds every week. It's on day and night, it's never never turned off. I don't know about the summer because I haven't been there. I spoke to one lady and she told me it was on during the summer also. One of the girls that works in the hotel used to come down to the kitchen because she couldn't stand the heat. I only wish we could complain about it. They could spend the money in a different way.

The atmosphere in our hotel's quite nice. They are quite helpful and they know whether you're in or out. If you ask them how to get to some place they can help you. I think if you don't cause trouble, they don't hassle you.

I didn't stay there at Christmas, but there was quite a lot of fighting, between girl and boyfriends, and the police were brought. A friend of ours, who went home, gave us the loan of her flat, which was fantastic. The children really enjoyed it, especially the kitchen. It was so nice having one again, and a sitting room so you could just sit down and relax. And they got really really settled: at about half six Douglas'd say, 'Mummy, put on my pyjamas,' and he'd go into the bedroom and stay in there. They were fantastic! My husband said he couldn't get over the difference in them. It's security, you know? You know here, every evening I have a carrier bag and I take my food down to the kitchen and come up again and . . . it was great.

We used to have a few friends in London, we've no relations. But since we came into bed and breakfast we seem to have lost contact with most of our friends – I think it's because we live so far away, and they're all in houses, and we're in bed and breakfast. There's some sort of a stigma attached to homelessness. You don't really want to tell people that you're in a hotel and people don't really understand, unless they're in the same circumstances. That's why I come to the Bayswater Centre, because listening to all the other girls, I can learn so much from them.

People don't realise what bad circumstances those people are living in, specially people with older children; they're all missing out on school. I'm sure it leaves a black spot on their life. A lot of the kids I know don't go to school. They're about 13 or 14, and they're just sitting. All this ought to be looked into and all this money spent on finding homes for these people. They should definitely build new homes. Why have people in bed and breakfast for two and a half years? They'd be saving money by giving flats to us people. If they'd put us into temporary accommodation, instead of bed and breakfast . . . money spent on bed and breakfast is just like throwing it down the river.

I come to the Bayswater Centre every day, snow, rain, regardless. If I didn't I'm sure I would talk to you differently. I'm sure I'd be having a nervous breakdown. I definitely wouldn't be able to sit all day in the room. It's fantastic that we have the Centre to come to. Otherwise I wouldn't be able to survive. They should build more of these centres in different areas for the homeless, because most people don't even know this place exists. We can cook here every day. A lot of the mothers chip in and we all cook something. So at least they get something to eat, which is good.

I was in the hotel three weeks before I found out about this place, and those three weeks were hell. Every evening when my husband came home I used to barge out of the door and say, 'You have them now.' I was very nervous, very short-tempered. It was just unbelievable what I went through in those three weeks. I would walk to the park – but you get sick of walking there because you can only stay there about an hour anyway. That was in October, and it was quite cold.

My husband leaves the house every morning at about six o'clock and he doesn't get home until about seven-thirty, so he doesn't really see much of the children. He works on Saturdays also, so he's just off on Sunday. We tend to go out all day, we go to the park, and I get a break. The only break I get during the week is when I go down and cook the meal in the evening – I'm about the only mother I can think of that looks forward to going cooking in the evening. I am, that is true!

I think I'd have come from Ireland anyway, it's better for my husband to be working. In our marriage anyway, there were an awful lot of ups and downs when he wasn't. We were continuously fighting, it just wasn't working out. There's no work whatsoever in Ireland. We were living in the country. I must say, for me it was lovely to be near my family. I miss all that. I could go to see them and I could take the children to the beach, but for him there was absolutely nothing. He was getting very, very depressed. I'm sure he'd have had a nervous breakdown.

My family didn't want us to leave. But I think they kind of understood it because in anybody's marriage, if you don't have an income you shouldn't live off the State. In Ireland, the State pays your rent but that's about it. We used to get £75 a week; it was impossible, because we were paying our car back out of that. From my mother-in-law and my mother, I used to get potatoes and vegetables. The rent was £20 a week and we had to get our own electric and then we had coal fires – I'll tell you, it was very hard at times.

In Ireland a lot of people are emigrating to the States, they're going illegally, specially with children – looking over their shoulders all the time, and wondering if they're going to be sent out of the country. I'd love to have gone, but the insecurity of it – when you're illegal, you're always looking, aren't you?

The depression is very bad in Ireland now, unemployment is very high and the job prospects are practically nil. Solicitors, doctors, all the professional people – they're all emigrating, all the school leavers. The whole of Ireland, even Dublin, a lot of people are leaving. They either come here or to the States. I lived in Southern Ireland, in County Kerry, which is a beautiful area.

Where I was living at home there was no young people. If we went out at night, socialising, it was all married couples and elderly people. No boys – I met my husband over here. It's got worse in the last few years – definitely – there's absolutely no young people. All the people I grew up with and went to school with, everybody we know, has emigrated. During the summer maybe it's not so bad, it's a bit livelier, because of tourism. They live on it. The government there is a joke. They think Maggie Thatcher is bad, but they're the pits. They'e not doing anything, really, for the young. They open up an awful lot of factories and they get an awful lot of grants but I think they're cutting down on these, and once the grant is withdrawn, factories close. In the area where I live there's about twelve factories closed down within three years. Once the grants had run out, everything closed down.

There are 12 of us in the family, and there are eight still at school. One sister, she lives in the UAE, one brother, he lives in New York. One of my sisters came over here – she's doing nursing in Manchester. The other sister's still at school. My parents – that's the saddest part. When we leave, they get very disheartened, because they know it'll be years before they see us again. They get very, very lonely. You can't leave a job if you want to, because you know you've no place else to go to. England's certainly better, definitely better.

When I spoke to Helen again, early in 1989, she told me she had spent six months in bed and breakfast. In the summer of 1988 she and her family were rehoused in a temporary housing association flat in Willesden, which they had furnished and decorated. Her husband was working in Docklands and she was looking forward to working again as soon as her sons were bigger. They were much happier, she said, although of course she had no idea how long they would be able to stay in the flat.

67

Maria and Deirdre

I met Maria and Deirdre in the waiting room at the Bayswater Families Centre, where they had come for advice. I decided to interview them together because they were close friends who had given each other a lot of support during their ordeal in the hotel.

Maria is 28, thin and fragile-looking. She is a Londoner who had well-paid office jobs until she became homeless. She is single but has lived with her boyfriend, Steve, for 11 years. As a single woman with no children she would not usually have been eligible for rehousing, but as both she and her boyfriend had a history of drug addiction and breakdown, they would have been considered 'vulnerable'.

When I first met Maria she was extremely nervous and made compulsive gestures with her hands all the time. The second time we met, with Deirdre in an Indian restaurant, Maria told me she was on tranquillisers. She sat very still and seemed zombie-like rather than tranquil. She kept apologising and was unable to eat; she could only drink fruit juice and coffee. As she and Deirdre talked, Maria frequently touched her friend across the table, as if to comfort her and be comforted. She and her boyfriend were about to move in to a housing association flat, after 14 months in bed-and-breakfast. Because the furniture grant no longer exists, and Maria didn't qualify for a furniture loan, she had no furniture at all to move in with. She read from notes she had made about her experiences.

Deirdre comes from Ireland. She is 23, with short, fair, wavy hair and calm grey eyes. Deirdre is a nurse and a trained counsellor. She nursed for five years before she became homeless in March 1988, two months before I met her. She has a two-year-old daughter, Anna, who at the time of the interview was living with her father, Tom, and his mother, because Deirdre couldn't cope with her in bed and breakfast. The hospital where she worked had told her she could have her job back any time. Deirdre's story shows how quickly families and careers are destroyed by the blight of homelessness. She was passionately concerned about the other people in the hotel, particularly Maria.

Deirdre: I became homeless when I came to England. I lived with a friend in Acton who then moved out. I found it very difficult to stay on my own in the flat. It was £175 a week, which I couldn't afford on my own when I was working. I found it difficult to feed my daughter, and to keep myself. So I went to see a social worker, Diane, and she told me to go bed-and-breakfast. I went to the Council, Ealing, and they put me in the White Leaf Hotel.

I've been there two months now; I found it very, very difficult with Anna. They're not very understanding towards people that have children. The owner isn't sympathetic either. He thinks you should be out working, he doesn't like people that are on Supplementary Benefit. He thinks that they're lazy. I want to go back to work but I can't, because I am on tranquillisers to try and keep myself steady.

When I first went into the hotel, I spent 14 solid days in my room, without speaking to anybody. I didn't even want to know my daughter, I was so depressed. At the end of it I felt like killing myself, and taking my daughter with me. I didn't want to live any more, I didn't see the reason for living. The only thing that brought me back was to think of my daughter. Also at that time I was six weeks pregnant, which wasn't helping a lot. The baby was wanted, but – I couldn't cope. I knew, with two children, it was going to be very, very hard. So I started doing things, like cleaning my room out and helping downstairs, talking to people, but it didn't help. That's one of my faults, taking on other people's problems, and everybody else's children, to avoid facing my own problems. I didn't want to face my own, so I helped with everybody else's. Plus when people know you're a nurse, they come to you, and knock on your door. People don't understand that you have problems, and you just can't take on everybody else's.

I was in the hotel seven weeks when I decided, that was it, I'll just take my own life. Couldn't stick it any more. So I went to see a doctor in Acton, he put me on tranquillisers, and I wanted to sleep. I was sitting downstairs and sleeping most of the time. I didn't want to live. My boyfriend, Anna's father, couldn't understand why I didn't want a relationship with him any more. I kept saying, 'Just take Anna off me! Because I just can't cope.'

I went to Social Services, and they tried to help me. Thursday last I really went to pieces, because Supplementary Benefit wouldn't give me any money. I had no money to feed Anna, I had no money to feed myself. When I went to the hotel owner he had no sympathy, no sympathy at all. He said to me, 'Well, if you can't afford to keep yourself you shouldn't be here.' He told me to keep Anna upstairs, because she

69

was playing in the lobby. Other people's kids play in the lobby. They have nowhere else at all. I felt as if he was singling me out.

I had a friend come to see me, so I went downstairs to get the iron. And the receptionist opened my shirt and made a pass at me. I told him I was going to phone the police, but I didn't want to get myself into trouble either, so I didn't. He would have thrown me out. I told the owner, and he wouldn't believe it. So then when my friend came, the receptionist said to him, 'You wait there, you can't go up to the room.' I mean, my daughter was up there. That was because Fitzroy's black, and also he's a policeman, so that didn't help either. That night the receptionist threatened to punch my face in. This fellow is Pakistani, yet he's got this thing against black men. He said, 'You like black fellows, you like policemen.'

I felt so small, so tiny, you know? As if he was putting me in a corner. I said, 'Why did you do that?' He said, 'You don't like me.' I said, 'I have no hatred for anybody. I'd take anybody's problems on – you know that.' Because he has sat, many a day, and told me his problems; I wouldn't repeat them to anybody.

I just felt so, so depressed. I went to my room and I cried. My daughter Anna couldn't understand it. I just couldn't stand any more. I rang the social worker the next morning and said, 'Would you please come and take Anna?' Anna is with Tom and his mother now.

Children are at risk in the hotel. There's an awful lot of things going on. I stated to Social Services: 'I'm *not* going to bring Anna back here. I mean my door doesn't close. If she goes out on the patio she can fall right down, there's a 16-foot drop. She can smash her head, or break her back. Last week they all had fleas and measles. Anna had bites from cockroaches. She went on Thursday. I missed her so much, I was crying, I was really depressed. And I had to say to Maria, 'You have to give me a tranquilliser to calm me down,' because I couldn't hold on any more. Even so, I was still very, very shaky, I couldn't control it. I had a shower, and I saw this cockroach coming from my shower. It was about this high. I don't know what way I felt: 'God, just take my life here and now, because I just can't keep it any more.' I got into bed and I had these awful pains, and I didn't know whether to tell Maria, I was so depressed. When I got up I was bleeding very, very heavily, so I had to go to the hospital. They said to me, 'I'm sorry, but your baby is coming away.' I felt awful. I would have been twelve weeks pregnant. If I had been looking after myself, looking after my daughter, I wouldn't have been in the state I was. If the hotel had been more responsible towards us, and sent in the Rentokil to do something about the place. Now I've lost two babies, I've lost the daughter I loved so much and the baby I was expecting. And I said to myself, Why go on? I mean, life isn't worth going on with, because I haven't got the people that I love. I'm going to see a psychiatrist. I feel as if I want to do something, I want to get out of that hotel.

I'm going to ask to change – somewhere that doesn't have fleas, and somewhere that I can relax. I mean everybody in there talks about Maria, talks about me. Plus, the management is so ignorant. My room was broken into, and there was money taken out of my purse, and other things taken. When I went down and explained, they said, 'It's your own tough luck.' Anyone can get into the rooms, they have the same key for every four doors. They don't care; as long as they're getting the money off the Council, they don't give a damn at all.

I was working until I came to live in the hotel eight weeks ago. I was working in Acton and for Ealing as well, but I couldn't continue it. It was too hard, because I was in the room all the time with Anna, and I couldn't sleep. I couldn't have got up at five o'clock in the morning. Also it was costing me so much. It's just crazy. I couldn't cope any more. I've been a qualified nurse now for three years. But before that, altogether, between a care assistant and an auxiliary, five years. It's a job that you can always have. It's the only job I'm trained for, I can't go out as a shop assistant. It's a job that I enjoy doing. If there's somebody ill in the hotel, I know I'm always there for them.

What I want is to have Anna back, a better hotel, and, I want to be myself again. I don't want to be somebody that's just in the hotel, looking after children, taking on everybody else's responsibilities. Once I lost my baby I went really downhill. I hadn't got my daughter, but I knew that I could rely on Maria. If she hadn't've been there I just would have stayed in my room in the hotel as I did at the beginning. The hotel management abuse you, as if you're dirt, and it isn't right. Because we are homeless, they treat you as if you've got a disease. The cleaners treat you like dirt as well.

I feel it's better if I do stay on the housing list, because of the benefit to us all. I am trying to break away from Tom. My mum died and he's been with me all through that. I know there's something between us because of Anna, but I feel so much for the feller I'm with now. He knows about Anna, he was with me when I lost the baby, and the baby wasn't even his, it was Tom's. He means more to me than anybody, except for Anna, he's been with me through hard times as well.

I can't remember how I met Maria. I think I'd been in the hotel about three weeks. The others keep themselves to themselves; they don't associate with our type.

71

Maria: I've had a good career, I have a lot of expensive clothes, I did have a very good life, once. We had a flat and Steven was working on the oil rigs, so that's how we afforded it. He had a very good job, trained as a surveyor for testing the soil of the beds. We've been together 11 years. I was an office manager for sales administration, I had a good job, travelled round the world too. So we had a lot of money and a good house; then Steven was made redundant, the oil rigs fell through. He was about 30 then, and it was a dreadful shock to him. And he's a very intelligent young man. He couldn't get another job. He tried as hard as he could. My salary couldn't cover the bills; we tried to hang on to the flat, and unfortunately we ran into so much debt that when we sold it, by the time we'd paid off the debts, the profit we'd made had gone. We had to live apart. He went to live with his sister in Putney and I went to live with a friend in Ealing. We couldn't bear to be apart, so I got us placed into bed-and-breakfast in January 1987. They said, 'You are emergency homeless; you'll only be in there six weeks and then you'll be put in a flat.' As soon as we moved in, Steven started taking heroin.

He had taken it previously, on and off. He started taking massive doses; he could not cope with the hotel. We never spoke to anyone. There were no cooking facilities, there were no fridges in the rooms, there was one bathroom to be used by 20 people. And he was unemployed, so all our money was going on his drugs. Our relationship fell apart – sex, everything. Then I started taking heroin, to try and understand. I hadn't, before. I wanted to get to his level; I did it to communicate with him. I ended up so depressed that I overdosed. Steven just happened to come back and managed to save me. It was about February last year.

I ended up in a mental hospital, St Bernard's, to be detoxed. I didn't expect Steve to come back. I'd planned it all, I took a load of Valium, and I knew that on top of the heroin it would kill me. I just thought, I don't want to live any more, I can't stop Steve – I'm addicted to Steve. I can't stop what's happening, I can't see any way out. My family have cut me off, my friends I see no longer, I see no one, I just stay in this room.

When I came out, Steve was still doing what he was doing. I had had treatment for severe depression and had been dried out, detoxed. So I started sleeping around, for comfort, because I was so lonely. But with the guilt feelings it didn't work out, because I love Steve, so I had a relapse, back on drugs.

June 87 I went to the toughest Drugs Rehab. there is, but it damaged me mentally so severely that I had another breakdown. It was severe group therapy: 40 people yelling at you telling you you're full of shit. It affected me very badly. After three weeks, the doctor diagnosed me as having to go into the hospital. Steven came to pick me up but instead of taking me to hospital he took me back home.

I came back and I went to bed and I did what I would call a slow suicide. I did not get out of bed to wash, didn't eat, I didn't answer the telephone. Steven was working, taking drugs intermittently, at the weekend. My weight dropped to about six and a half stone. I'd lost the will to live, totally. I was cut off from everybody, there was no one I could relate to in the hotel. I was like a zombie, really, I couldn't cope with anything. Steve wasn't giving me any love or support.

I had no friends at all, just Steve, who didn't communicate. Finally he dragged me to a hospital in Harrow, to a psychiatrist who started looking after me. It wasn't doing much good. Then we were thrown out of the hotel overnight because the police found out we were using drugs.

In the next hotel I did the same as Deirdre: I locked myself in my room. I was terrified someone would find out. Then I found out about the needle exchange caravan next to St Mary's. I dragged myself down there and I said, 'Look. I've had a positive cervical smear. I was diagnosed three years ago.' I'd done nothing about it and I thought, if I don't I'm going to die, and it's a waste. Because I do know, deep inside me, there's still a strong girl. They took me to a clinic at St Mary's where I was admitted, and got operated on for cervical cancer. They had me tested for H I V and all the tests were negative, thank God, they cleared all that up. The Dangerous Drugs Unit (DDU) started Steve on a methadone reduction programme; they also put me on a reduction programme, so that I wouldn't relapse. They're now counselling us together; they have helped us enormously. We don't talk together, outside the counselling, but when we are faced, me and Steve and the counsellor, the truth comes out.

We don't talk to each other otherwise. He doesn't make love to me at all. He hasn't had any work for a long time. I used to be a very strong girl, very independent, I used to do acting, and, of course, living with someone who's been in bed and just living in squalor for months and months and months – he's lost all respect for me. Deep down I know that one of the roots of the problem is that Steve isn't good for me, because he's one of those people who will always use heroin, on and off. He'll come off for a year, he has done, he's stopped for two years, and then he'll come on again. He can't give me what I need. I would say it's an obsessional relationship.

I don't know how it happened with Deirdre, we just got talking, and I spilt the beans. I would never have dared do that before, because there's so much gossip around. I told Deirdre what was really happening. Deirdre warned me, she said, 'Be careful, Maria. Because people are noticing.' Then I went up to her in tears and told her what was going on. In fact it was only yesterday that I told her I myself was also on a reduction programme – not because I use it like Steve but because we're going through such problems that if Steve was to go and get heroin, you know, I'd be so tempted . . .

I never touched drugs in my life, before this. I never drank before, I never thought of suicide. I was a very strong, independent girl. Now I've become totally dependent on Steve, I've become agoraphobic, I've become like a little girl. I can't function on my own any more. I can inside, but when Steve's around I just become like a little girl.

It's because he's become the sole person in my life, and I've been in bed and breakfast for 14 months. I've become like a child. I can't do anything any more, I can't cross the road, I can't go shopping, I can't write a letter. I can't do anything without Steve. It's ridiculous.

My intention is to do the flat up, and get the same job again. I've got the flat through a housing association, and I'll go and tell them the truth; that Steve is still doing what he's doing. I intend asking them for another flat so I can live on my own, and I'm sure they'll give it to me, if they know what's happening with Steve. It will be very difficult for me to break with Steve, we've been together for 11 years. But I think, once I go back to doing my amateur dramatics and doing the job I used to do – I did a lot of plays – then, I think, I'll change. I seriously do.

The sad thing is, there's no one in my life, except Deirdre and Steve. That's it – apart from my stepmother. My father married again. They're in Gloucestershire. So in London, the only person I have to talk to, is Deirdre which isn't fair, because I feel very guilty. The other day I collapsed in tears about something trivial; I'd made a cock-up of some money. Bed and breakfast – it's broken me down. I'm totally ashamed to admit it, you know – it's all very difficult, upsetting, to explain.

I went to my mother and I told her the truth. Because I'm an honest person. She doesn't want to know. As soon as she heard the truth, her attitude was, 'Well then, you leave Steve.' It's not as easy as that. I can't explain it. He's all I have left – after 11 years – the roles are reversed. Instead of me keeping him off heroin, I've become a little girl that has to be looked after. Do you understand? I can't just leave him. Where am I going to go? I'm not strong enough to live by myself. We'll probably go to the flat together, and slowly I'll rebuild back to being what I was. And then – wham! I'll go.

Deirdre: Maria's such a good friend. Also, she helps me and I help her. She wants a baby, I have a baby. Being with Anna, she talked to her, while I did the washing. That helped her and it helped me. In that square box room, sitting there day by day on my own, I'm with somebody I know that I can trust. I will miss her an awful lot. But as I sit here Maria, I'll come and see you. I keep saying to her, 'Look, I do want to befriend you, but be careful.' Because the person that owns the hotel, he would throw them out over drugs. He has approached me three times, because I am a nurse: I said, 'Look, Maria isn't on drugs. She's a girl that has an awful lot of problems. Leave her alone! Stay off her back!'

I feel as if you're in this box, and the box is closed tight and you can't get out. I just feel, get me out of here, whatever way, just *get me out*! Half the times I've had to keep the door open, to see who was going past, so I knew that the feeling was only a dream, there are other people in the hotel as well as me.

Maria: It breaks down some people quicker than others. It breaks down everyone eventually. Everyone in that hotel has some way of coping with it; they either turn to drink or drugs or sex or prostitution or gambling. Everyone there has a secret.

Deirdre: One girl that had a mentally handicapped little boy was in her room with the children and her ceiling fell through. It's just lucky the little girl wasn't in the cot – it actually came into it. The manager said, she had to stay in this room. He was going to make her stay there, with a mentally handicapped child in that room, full of dampness, clay, cement, everything. And her sister next door, her ceiling was falling the same way.

In my room I had a hole. The shower unit upstairs was leaking into the bedroom. I had to go and report it, specially since there was a baby there, and I said, 'Look, the ceiling is leaking, it's bad for the child. Because the child could have a bad chest or anything. It's leaking down on to the bed.' 'Well let her sleep on it.'

Ealing Council has had six different reports. Someone from the Housing Department came down. The day before, the owner had the hotel all cleaned up. The Council woman said it was fine. She only sees what she wants to see. She said, 'Have you noticed anything that isn't meant to be noticed?'

Maria: She wanted her to split on other people.

Deirdre: I said, 'I'll show you what I've seen. Come up to Room 204. Come up to Room 101. We're living in diabolical situations.' 'Oh let me see!' she said.

When I went up to 204, he had had the floor done by then. I said, 'A mentally handicapped boy has to sleep in here.' Do you know what she said to me? 'Where's the dust?' I said, 'He has had it cleaned! Can you not understand?' She says, 'What's your profession?' I said, 'I told you, I've been a nurse for five years. And here I'm a resident counsellor. These people don't need counselling in here, they need psychiatric help because of what's going on.'

She did nothing. She won't, because, as far as we know, in February of next year we will all be out of the White Leaf Hotel. The owner is going to abuse us in any way he can, because Ealing Council aren't going to use it any more.

Maria: I live off £32 Supplementary Benefit. But I'm not getting anything at the moment because I messed it up. My boyfriend has now spent two days from 8.15 to 5.30, at Lisson Grove trying to get us some money. We've had no money at all. We're living on pasta and butter and cheese. When people are in dire straits they help each other out.
Deirdre: In a place like the White Leaf you have to. I can go to any hospital and get a job. But I don't want to go back yet.
Maria: That's the other thing. It's nearly two years now since I've worked. I've tried to get jobs, but when you say you're living in bed and breakfast, there's no way they'll give you a job. And you can't lie about it, because they find out. Even when I did get a job for a couple of weeks, I could hardly keep it up. I couldn't sleep, because people were making a noise all night; I couldn't iron my clothes on the floor – it's just too much.
Deirdre: You haven't got any privacy because – there's no facilities for anybody. You've got cooking facilities which close at half seven, eight o'clock. Younger children go to bed at around half seven. Those children run around during the day with dirty nappies because the mothers just don't want to be bothered getting up. They do become zombies because they just can't cope. I've had people ask me, 'Could you prescribe tranquillisers?'

I said to this psychiatrist, 'It's only because I can help Maria and the other people that I am keeping myself up.' Because at night now when I go to bed, I'm not worrying about me, I'm saying, 'Well, is Maria going to be all right with Steve? And is Mandy going to be all right with her two? When I did counselling for a year, I had so many people coming to me, and now I know what it feels like, to be in their situation. I know, I can feel the hurt that they've had, and I know what they're feeling inside. Before, I didn't. I feel I can give them more. I know how disgusting it is to be in bed-and-breakfast.

Early in 1989 I tried to trace these two young women. Maria was still at the flat she and her boyfriend had moved to, but I was unable to find out what had happened to Deirdre.

Shelly

Many Bangladeshi families are homeless. Under the old terms of the Immigration Act, Commonwealth citizens who settled in Britain before 1973 are allowed to bring their wives and children here. However, in May 1988 ten homeless Bangladeshi families who had been reunited under these terms – 66 people – were declared 'intentionally homeless' by Liberal–controlled Tower Hamlets Council (see also Mary Tester's interview). The Bishop of Stepney housed these families in church halls on an emergency basis. In the same month new Immigration legislation was passed. This prevents Commonwealth citizens who settled in Britain before 1973 from bringing their families to this country, unless they can prove they can support themselves without help from the State.

The head of each of the households involved in the Tower Hamlets case had worked and paid taxes in the United Kingdom for at least 25 years (like Shelly's father). Tower Hamlets' decision is important because it will make it easier for other local authorities to evict homeless families, and will undermine the Homeless Persons' Act.

As the latest large group of immigrants – and the last, if this Government has its way – Bangladeshis have suffered disproportionately from discriminatory housing policies.

Shelly Miah came from Bangladesh when she was six. She is now 20, married with two little girls aged two and a half years and eight months. Her husband works as a waiter and she used to work in a supermarket. She lived in bed-and-breakfast hotels for seven months when her elder daughter, Sabrina, was a baby, before being rehoused in a two-bedroomed flat in Paddington.

Shelly joined the toy library a year ago but wasn't able to come in as she was housebound with the children. I had only spoken to her on the telephone before I went to interview her. Her flat is in a row of crumbling Victorian houses in Paddington which have been converted into a block of flats with ingenious awkwardness. A sign outside announced 'Westminster City Council'. Inside, the building was smelly and depressing, with dirty red linoleum floors and crumbling yellow stucco walls. In the lift graffiti advised me to PISS OFF. The lift only went up to the second floor, where I got lost in bleak corridors marked only by fire doors and ancient-looking fire extinguishers. After ten minutes wandering around looking for Shelly's flat I felt quite trapped. I found it at last, through several fire doors and up a flight of stairs. She welcomed me at the door, a dignified woman in a sari with a lively, expressive face. She wore her glossy black hair in a bun and spoke English in a husky voice with a Bengali accent.

Shelly's flat is spacious but very shabby. In her big living room I met her two children, her cousin, a girl of about her age, and another relative, a boy of 13. Shelly was pleased to see me but nervous at first. She soon relaxed, obviously enjoyed talking and laughed a lot during the interview.

I was living with my mother, and I got pregnant with my first child. It's a very small flat, near Victoria. When she was born, I had to go to the Homeless because there was no room for me. When I first went in there, I went straight from the hospital. They put me in the first hotel and it was terrible; really like an attic; the window was broken. So I just came down and told the Council. Then they looked for another place; it was also a very tiny room, it was okay but there were no cooking facilities. I stayed there for about two months, then I had to move because I don't like eating out. I just don't trust people, how they cook! Then they moved me to Berkeley Court. Really small room. I don't like the hotel, it's really dirty too. The bathroom wasn't clean, the carpet wasn't clean, and the net on the window was there for ages and ages. They hadn't washed it. It wasn't nice at all, I didn't like staying in the hotel, specially at night time. My husband wasn't working. I used to tell him to go out, most of the time. He was working afterwards, after a few months. Sometimes he used to come late, and we used to hear fights, arguments next door. So many drunk people, and especially prostitution. Women used to bring so many different kind of men in – I don't know if it was prostitution. One day in our hotel a man upstairs brought in a prostitute. His wife was out – she went somewhere for a week. There were three men altogether. The man next door, he was very good man, went upstairs: 'In this hotel families are living, why did you bring the prostitute in?' They were going to call the police, but the prostitute went out.

There were plenty of cockroaches. I was terrified of them. I used to be out most of the day, I used to come in just to sleep. When I used to go into this room I used to think, this is a prison. I used to cry to myself. I think people living in a hotel long-term probably go mental. I find it myself, and I'm a very capable woman. You can't really move. If you move backwards, something falls. You have to keep the child in the cot; you can't put a child down, the carpet is filthy. Even if you put her down she can't really move. She had to be in the cot, for seven months.

I don't think the Council should do this. For the amount of money they pay to the homeless people to live in a hotel, they could build temporary flats. They were paying a hundred and something for the room. That's disgusting. Just for one room. I hate being homeless. I don't think I would become homeless unless I had to. You think you will never move out of the room. There was a woman downstairs with two children living in one room and she'd been there for two years.

I kept going to that office to see my social worker. She was very nice, and I kept going to her. I had so much depression. I never told nobody – I used to cry to myself, sitting in there.

There was food under your bed, food in the drawers. The shower was in the middle of your room, it just stood out, stupid. There was a curtain, but you felt horrible, sort of unusual and unhealthy. Plus the toilets – oh my goodness! The cleaner cleaned it, but so many people used one loo, and I used to hate it. I used to clean it myself, then I used to go in. Because people just used to do everything everywhere and I used to feel sick. One night, do you realise, I had to hold myself in? I didn't want to go to the toilet; I used to feel sick.

So many people used to look at you; you don't have anything private there. People wanted to mix with you. I didn't want to mix . I didn't really like the other people. There was a woman downstairs who used to leave her child in the middle of the night – she was about five or six – and go out and enjoy herself with men. I did make friends, because I had to. If you don't make friends, if you don't talk to anybody, you'll go mental.

The kitchen was downstairs; by the time you cook and you come up you're tired, you don't want to eat. That's why I have lost so much weight, I just went off food. I lost between half and one stone when I was in the hotel. If your husband's out and there's a fight next door, it's terrifying, because they're drunk. There's one lock on the door. Say someone breaks in, there's nothing we can do. There was a buzzer in the room; that was the only thing that made me stay there.

I decided to go to the hotel because my mother didn't have much room. My sister, a teenager, had to live in the living room. There were three small bedrooms. I had one with my husband. There's my mother, my father, my two brothers and my sister, so it was terrible, you know, they didn't have freedom. I could hardly put the baby's cot in the room. So I had to go to the hotel. I was 18 when Sabrina was born. I got married in 1985. People had said there were one or two problems in the hotels, specially with the cooking. But unless you go there, you think, they're coping, they're happy. But if you go there for yourself, you know how depressing it is.

Before Sabrina was born I was working in a supermarket. My family came to England in 1975 or 76. My dad was here, we came to join him. I've been back to Bangladesh twice; it's very nice, but once you've been brought up here it's very difficult for you to get used to it. Some people are very shy; my sister is very quiet, you can hardly get a word out of her. She came when she was ten months. Whereas me, I'm very open. To a Bangladeshi, I'm more of a Westerner. To someone Western, I'm more Bangladeshi, I'm in the middle really. Piggy in the middle. My mum's not all that glad we came here. But me – I like going to Bangladesh, it's a very nice family, all the relatives. But I don't think I could live there for ever.

I think everybody always has a dream of going back. They want to die in their own land. That's the older generation. The new generation are more likely to want to stay here. They've been brought up here, they were born here, they think this is their home. With me, at the end of the day, I don't know where I would settle.

My husband is working as a waiter. He doesn't like this country, I think he would like to go back. In our country if you have land you can live on your land. You have more freedom. But over here, if you don't go to work, ten minutes later you get told off, you get sacked. Getting a giro from Social Security – I've just been with my cousin. Terrible! I don't like it, going there. Being on the dole is terrible. It's hard work. They look at you like you're using them, you're taking charity.

I've met women who've come from the villages and ended up in hotels. You think, when you're coming to England, it'll be heaven. When they come and see the hotels, they feel like going back. They don't know what they came for. They complain to their husbands – 'Why did you bring me? I don't want to come to this place. You said it was going to be nice.' They expect a big house, everything new, plenty of money. They expect their children to be educated to a better standard.

Some very young girls who come to Britain come from very poor families. They get married to older husbands. I don't think they get any choice. They *have* to get married; there's no Social Security, no nothing out there. If they come from a poor family at first their parents support them, and then after that the husband will support them. Nowadays

81

most girls get primary education, just basic Bengali, basic writing and reading, that's it. Some girls get a very, very good education: you see woman lawyers in Bangladesh now, magistrates and doctors. But they're from a rich family because a lot of money is needed just to get to school, and then college. Most people who live in hotels are from the villages and they don't have all that education. Few of them have secondary school, one or two of them come from college; very few.

A man who has a job in England comes back to the village: 'Oh I'm from England, I've got a house down there,' or, 'I've got a restaurant.' Nobody's coming to check over here. If he lives in Bangladesh they'll check. So he goes up to the girl: 'I'm marrying her, I'm going to take her with me.' Her parents think, 'That's good. At least she will be off my hands. At least she will be able to help me.' The girl doesn't have any choice, because if she lets her parents down, she will feel awful. She's living off her parents; she has to get married. I find it very sad; I don't think I would be able to do that. If a girl refuses that's it, she'll get married to a poor man. Girls get married in their early teens, from 14, 15, up to 20. Age is one thing nobody records on a book. If somebody wants to get married and the girl is about 19, her parents probably say she's about 16. They don't want to put too much age on the girl. They have a very hard life. Life is short. Even though I am brought up in this country, I don't think too much about enjoying myself. To a Bengali girl, her husband, her children, her relatives, are very important, come first.

Frankly speaking I find that in England they give people too much freedom, they get spoilt. Everything's getting out of hand. Some of these people on drugs, they hardly give a damn about their parents. That's what upsets me. Because in our country, they follow the West. I don't know why they follow the West – you never follow the East, do you? I think we have our own good culture which is respectable, and looking after the elderly is very nice. And looking after a relative who is not well off.

I'm still very close to my mother. She comes to see me and she phones me every day. Specially with the grandchildren. She works in a school, she teaches Bengali. She is okay in England, but she would like to go back to Bangladesh, one day. We have been brought up here, I can talk to you any time, I'm not shy, and I know what you're thinking, and you know what I'm thinking. My husband thinks I'm 20 but I still have the mind of a child. When I speak with you I think I'm more grown-up. I learned English when I was six. I wrote an autobiography. I wrote all my experiences. That was before I got married. How I came to this country, how my father used to write to us. The funny thing is, when I was small I used to think England was up in the sky! Do you know why? The plane used to go up there! I never saw a plane close up until I went to the airport. The plane was so high in the sky I thought it was so small, how did the parents fit on that plane? I used to think they had some kind of machine that made them so small! I didn't know there was any such thing as England, or Great Britain, only London.

I grew up in a village and my father used to come to visit. He used to stay six or seven months, and when his money ran out he used to go back to England. It was very difficult for us when he left but we had our grandfather. He used to keep a shop.

When I was small we just used to use pants to go swimming. When I first came I remember they took me swimming. And the teacher told me to put on swimming trunks, but I just had my underpants on. I didn't have any swimming trunks. They let me go swimming in my underpants. And jelly. The first time I saw jelly I thought, What's that wobbling? At school they told me to eat it; and the spaghetti! I used to think it was worms they were eating. I had some problems with the language, but I learned it very quickly. At my time, 1976, there weren't many Bengalis in this country. I was the first Bengali everywhere, every school I went to.

They used to tease me. Now there are so many people, they're used to Asian, Black, and Chinese; they're in a multiracial area and they grow up. Sometimes I was unhappy, I used to feel very lonely, but I had a few friends.

There wasn't bad racism in the hotels. I think the women who couldn't speak English had a hard time, and everybody looked at Asian people, like they were refugees or something. To me they were friendly, because I could speak English. I just went around speaking to everybody. They all wanted to take me to the Homeless to talk, or take me to the DHSS, but I find it very hard. I don't like going to the DHSS, I find it really embarrassing. They look at you in such a way, as though you're so helpless.

Being homeless is terrible, it's – being less of everything. I was in the hotel seven months; to me it was seven million years. When they told me I had a flat, I nearly fainted! I jumped! When I came and saw this place, I didn't want to come. But then again I had to come because they said, 'You've got only one choice.' If I had said no, they would have made me wait another year. I couldn't do that, I would have gone mental there.

Jenny

All the other homeless interviewees were women whom I had met at the toy library. Jenny, however, telephoned me at home one evening, sounding breathless and incoherent. She said she was writing a book and had to talk to me. Jenny still has the accent and inflection of the convent school she left ten years ago. We met for supper in a restaurant but she was unable to eat, and tired, as she had been working all day in a supermarket. Jenny is 27, divorced, with a six-year-old daughter. In the past she had a drug problem, and this was one of the causes of her homelessness.

I had a divorce case. I'd lived in London for seven years and I left my job and I went right downhill. I became unhealthy, depressed. I had one child, called Antonia. At the time she was two. So I went up to Scotland, where my parents lived, and I stayed with them for three months and it didn't work out at all, because I hadn't lived with them since I was 16. And before that I'd been at boarding school for ten years, so it was a very distant sort of relationship, really.

Then I got a little flat in Scotland, privately rented from a woman who was very feminist – I mean she was all for giving flats to women with children, which is unusual. So there we were, and while we were there I got a new boyfriend, who was a Canadian.

I came down to London because of this divorce case. I had to go to the Royal Courts of Justice for the custody, so I had to come down – plus Peter, my boyfriend, had moved down to London for work. So I thought, it's time for a holiday. This was in August 1986. I arrived in London, we stayed with him, and I stayed here for three weeks instead of two. Then I got a phone call from Scotland from Pete's brother, saying that he'd walked past my flat, and all my belongings were lying on the pavement, and the local tinks were having a great time taking all they wanted. I was flummoxed. I had all kinds of antique rugs, all my paintings were originals, all done by friends of mine. The landlady herself was never out of the auctions, all the valuable things I know she kept. The stuff she put out on the street and the stuff his brother managed to salvage – I mean I got a few black bin bags full of stuff, and I didn't want what was there, it was rubbish.

My daughter was with me in London. My parents hadn't spoken to me for nearly two years. I went off the rails when I left school and stayed off the rails for ages. I had no friends in Scotland, bar Peter. I had no social life, no career, nothing going for me up there. So I thought, what am I going to do? I won't take the landlady to court because this divorce case had been going on for nearly five years and I'd had enough of courts. I wanted to get on with life. Antonia was due to start school in four weeks, so I made the decision to stay in London. And the landlord of the place where my boyfriend was staying said to me, 'You must go to the Homeless.'

Now the Homeless put me into the Seavan Hotel, which is in Prince's Square, and we stayed there two months, just me and Antonia. But of course Peter was with me a lot because I was pretty lonely, quite frankly. All kinds of rules and regulations about people leaving, but I'm not at boarding school any more and I'm not in prison. Then I started Antonia at school. So life was beginning again. And one day at the Seavan Hotel, Westminster Council phoned up and said, 'Look, we're moving you to a new hotel that's just opened.'

All this time Westminster have been debating whether or not I'm legally entitled to be housed by any of the London councils. My landlady in Scotland was very lucky, because I hadn't lifted a finger. I'm trying to cope with things down here. In my opinion she's a crook, I just can't be bothered with her. All right, I've lost everything, I'm not going to get it back. That happened in August 1986. We're now in February 1988. The Council still can't make up their minds whether they're going to house us.

We've been in this hotel now for one year, four months, and miserable about it. Work, thank God, keeps me sane. I got my job in March last year. It means we can live a little bit more normally than on the dole. I've got one room, two single beds and a fridge. We've got a shower and a loo, which is wonderful; I would hate to share a communal bathroom. I'm very creative. I'm an artist, I like writing, I enjoy cooking – but I can't cook there. I never know from one day to the next whether we're going to be staying or going. Four times in the past three months the Council have said categorically, 'You're out in two days.' And they've offered no alternative but to come and pick up a ticket to go back to Scotland, where I've got no connections at all. I've got parents there, but my parents and I have hardly spoken in the last decade. I only lived there for 18 months. I've lived in London for about eight years. Every threat I've had from the Council, John Maclean up at the Law Centre has acted, and stopped them. He's got a barrister who thinks I ought to take the Council to court. It's a nightmare.

There's lots more – like the attitude of the employees in the hotel to the residents. I've been threatened with being thrown out on so many different occasions – God, in the last year and a half I've got to know the staff as well as I've got to know my own family. And *they* were horrible. The staff are young, they're immature, they're foul-mouthed, and the only people they ever treat with any kind of regard are crazy. There are mental patients in the hotel, there are plenty of alcoholics. They put you off your breakfast. I manage with Antonia miraculously. She's an amazing little thing.

There was a lady who moved in the same day as I did, and her child was the same age as Antonia and her school was 200 yards away from Antonia's. So when I started work I paid her £20 a week to pick Antonia up, take her home, give her some tea and wait until I got back. And this worked out until she was rehoused in Croydon three weeks ago. Now there's a mother at Antonia's school, and I've got the same deal going with her now, so I've been extremely lucky. I'm working from nine till seven or eight o'clock at night. It's a long day . . .

What the councils don't seem to understand is that I'm a tax-paying, rate-paying, rent-paying, sane, hardworking person, willing to give to this society of London as much as I can. I'm getting treated like an illegal immigrant in my own country. I'm scared, because I can't honestly see it's going to get any better.

I want nothing to do with the DHSS again for the rest of my life. I pity everyone who has to go to the DHSS. But it's mainly the councils and it's the way the system runs; they make you put your trust in someone. 'This is your caseworker.' When your caseworker gives you a hard time and sends you away, and you try and find out exactly why, you just get told it's his seniors, and he can't do anything about it.

I've tried to rent privately and it's a bloody con; they don't want children. They don't want animals, but they'd rather have an animal than a child. So I'm at my wits' end now. I'm slowly beginning to think I'm losing this battle. It's like being in limbo for two years, nearly. Antonia's just an angel. It's in her nature to survive it all, children are like that. I'd have a football team if I was rich, I love children, I think they're marvellous.

Can I give you a really shocking example, that happened this morning? The childminder who lives near Antonia's school has got a little girl of six, the same age, Tammy. On Antonia's birthday, last November, she had three children to her birthday party and Tammy stayed the night. We just popped them into the one bed, and they had a bath together, they were really happy. I asked the manager of the hotel, due to Antonia's birthday, could Tammy stay and have breakfast with us the next morning? And he said yes, which was great. Last night it happened again, because it was Tammy's mother's birthday and she was going for a drink. It went very, very well indeed until this morning, when I took them down to breakfast, having informed the manager she was there. The children had sat themselves at the dining-room table before I came in and they were sitting there, all bright-eyed and bushy-tailed, and I asked them which cereals they wanted. And this skinhead who works there, he's awful, he's an idiot, came over to the table and said, 'I'm not serving you.' I said, 'Why not?' He said, 'You're not allowed to bring visitors down to the breakfast room.'

I said, 'But wait a minute, Terry, this is no visitor, this is Tammy and she's only six. Besides, I've paid rent here for seven months, and I had to be at work at seven in the morning at one point, so I wasn't at breakfast.' I said, 'I'm not eating into your profits, Terry, but if it makes you feel better, don't give me anything, give my breakfast to Tammy.' Terry put his hand on his hip in front of the two children and said, 'Do you really think I give a fuck?' in a very loud voice. I said, 'Terry, if you don't, why are you working here? You're a moron.'

Then the housekeeper came up to me and she said, 'Really, Jenny, we can't give the child food this morning because if the other guests see us feeding visitors they'll be bringing all their friends down to breakfast.' I said, 'She's not a visitor, she's an infant. It's snowing outside, you can't send them to school without their breakfast.' She goes, 'Jenny, we just can't do it, because if we do we're just giving ourselves a whole lot of hassle.'

It was all too much, I just said to the children, 'Come on, upstairs.' Half the people there don't even go down for breakfast. And their little faces! Oh my God! Inside, I was in complete turmoil. I took them upstairs and gave them jam sandwiches and lemonade, which was all I had, and walked them to school. And do you know what Tammy said? As we left the hotel she went, 'Anita's (her auntie) is the only place I can stay.' She picked up she wasn't wanted there because they wouldn't give her any food. That's just one tiny example and things like that happen almost daily.

I said to Westminster, 'I don't want a council place. Put me on the Housing Association list, or do one of your mortgages, I've got enough money to pay.' I'm running out of ideas, I don't know what to do. The only way private landlords will give me a flat is through a company let, and I can't get one. The best thing that could happen would be that Westminster would stop playing the ass and realise I'm willing to pay rent. I'm not going to sit back and wait for the Council to pay my rent. I'll even pay a Council mortgage, if they'll sell me one of their properties. That's really the best thing that could happen. I'm dying to get out of that hotel. I'm now the longest resident there.

The people next to me, take it from me, both use cocaine. To the extent that when they're coming down they get really, really angry, violent. One child. They beat each other up like crazy. The man isn't supposed to be there at all. The woman cries like a wounded animal, up to four hours a night, between say six and ten at night. One particular night, a couple of weeks ago, he threatened me because I buzzed down to the manager. I said, 'Come up and listen. And if you think I'm being unreasonable, go away again. But otherwise, please ask them to shut up.' Because Antonia was upset, she couldn't sleep. The walls are paper-thin. Instead of covering for me, he knocked on their door and said, 'Room 311 complained.' The guy was outside my door, kicking the door, saying, 'I'm going to stick you in the belly if you ever complain to the governor again.' This was about nine, Antonia was awake, she was crying.

A week ago, these two had been at it hammer and tongs, and Antonia was beginning to fret because it was violent. So I phoned down and said, 'Listen, I don't want the same trouble as last week, all I want is for you to come and sit with me in my room.' In the time it took for them to come up, the noise increased to such a pitch that I gave two thumps on the wall. Then I heard this terrible crash, like he was trying to come through the wall. Then my door went, and he said, 'If I ever see your face, I'm going to stick this knife right in your belly.' This was the second threat in a matter of weeks. I thought, Oh no, my first instant feeling was, I'm never going out of my door again. Then I thought, To hell with it. I opened my door and leaned out and said, 'Here's my face: now what are you going to do about it?'

The guy was standing there, he was only as big as I am, blazing with rage, waving his arms around. And it wasn't for quite a few minutes that I realised he did in fact have a knife in his hand. He was waving it around, right under my chin, and it was very, very sharp and shiny. It never touched me really but just skimmed my throat. At that point I just shut the door. I said, 'The only thing that I want you to do is to stop making so much noise. You have a child. I have a child.'

Then the staff came up, and the housekeeper came and sat with me for half an hour. If I'd called the police they wouldn't have been interested. I don't want to leave the room, because when we moved in, it was brand-new; the carpet was brand-new, it's my room. I wouldn't like to move into someone else's room.

I reckon if I'd stayed in Scotland the Council would have rehoused me. They've got a lot of flats – but you've got to see them! Scottish slums at their very worst. I wouldn't go there if they paid me a million dollars. Same as I wouldn't go in a council place in London.

My father's a diplomat; he worked for the United Nations for nearly 30 years. They've got the house in Scotland, five bedrooms, and another flat with five bedrooms, a house in the Orkney Islands with four bedrooms. They know what's happening. But I'm on my own, Jack. I'm 27 now. I haven't had a penny off them. My brother's actually five years older than me, and they send him regular cheques. They love me, I'm sure they wish things could have been better between us. I said to them, 'Look, if you can't accept me, then there's no damned way I'm going to split Antonia in two.' Seeing them would lend an aspect to her life that was slightly – I was going to say upmarket, but genteel is much better. My mother was quite heartbroken. We saw her at Christmas and she said, 'You're denying your child civilisation.' All they do is occasionally say, 'How's it going?'

The last ten years have been incredibly difficult. Since I left school at 16 – after ten years in a convent. I left bloody-minded, and I just made mistake after mistake. I first moved up to Scotland because my parents said, 'Look, Jenny, you're not well. Come up and live with us for two years.' That was in 1984, when Antonia was two. In fact they came down to England. They stayed with me for two weeks down in Devon. I was sitting in a caravan with them for two weeks and talking. They didn't want a hotel room, they wanted to sit in a caravan because it was more private. It was very strange. Out of season in a caravan in Devon. Talking to them for *two weeks*, every night late into the night.

They were trying to be sympathetic, 'Please call us Mum, please call us Dad.' It was kind of making amends. After two weeks they said, 'Right, get all your bags packed, now. We're going to take Antonia up in the car, there's your train ticket.' They sent all my luggage up, and I was just like a child. It was follow, follow, follow. It was Custer's Last Stand as a family. it was their last offer, and it was their first offer, if you know what I mean. They wanted us both dreadfully. I think they were lonely as well. They were both retired, they were losing a lot of their identity because their children were gone, and there I was in real need and they wanted to be able to help, which was wonderful. Anyway, I went up to Scotland and things broke down irretrievably. I mean horrifically. When I left it was under a big black cloud.

At the time, there was a drugs baron in Scotland that had been given twelve years in gaol. One of the reasons I was so ill before, was because I was dating his brother. He had gone up to Scotland and dug up a pound of uncut heroin from Pakistan, in a big, thick plastic bag. By the time this pound had vanished, I had a habit like nobody's business. I was smoking it and putting it up my nose. And then we were on the street. I needed the stuff and this was really the big fall, the big crash. Then I was using a needle, because it was cheaper, because you got the effect quicker – all such a load of rubbish! One of the reasons that I became so ill was that I contracted Hepatitis B. And I didn't even know I had it at the time; I was just really at the end of my rope. And I also overdosed on Valium, by accident. I was on holiday in Devon trying to wean myself off. I had only just told my parents, so they were really furious and flew down to Devon.

After the overdose, the welfare worker moved us into Westward Ho with a family who had flats and rooms, and they were going to put us into a flat in a couple of weeks. They were also assessing me. It was while I was there that my parents came down. They did realise before then, because my ex-husband, whom I left, had gone to gaol. He's doing a six-year sentence for heroin dealing.

I had to tell them when that happened. I used to pretend he was in the pub, in the bathroom, everywhere – but he was actually in gaol. They'd been through a lot of bullshit with me.

When I went up to Scotland I wasn't taking heroin; I genuinely wanted to stop. This was what the welfare worker in Devon could tell, the minute he looked at me. I'd got in touch with Nigel, my boyfriend, in Scotland; when my parents found out it was just *the end*. I wasn't taking it, but I was seeing him. I might as well have been taking it, as far as they were concerned. He wasn't taking it at the time either; he was living with his parents, I was living with mine. But the fact that I'd gone to see him again was just – 'Sorry honey, it's him or us.' And I said, 'Well, if you're going to put me in that kind of situation I'll have him, because you're really making me feel quite sick.' So I got hold of a friend, she put me up on a floor and within a week, I was in a flat. I haven't touched it since 1984. I wouldn't do it again. I'd rather you shot me, I wouldn't take it.

I've had a lot of years where I just rotted, mentally and physically. So I'm driving myself now, I'm really working hard – I got off it completely on my own. I didn't want to go down on medical records. This was the irony of it all. I didn't want to become registered, to get methadone, because it's such a thing against you. I don't know what I'm going to tell Antonia, some time in the future.

So, ultimately, I'm doing my penance now. In fact I do think like a Catholic, although I'm not one. In the end, it did go down on record, because when I arrived up in Scotland I got this kind of paralysis and it was found I had Hepatitis B. I was completely arthritic from my head to my toes for about three months. I couldn't switch on lights, open doors, turn on taps – I was in an awful state. My mother was so embarrassed, she thought it was something to do with coming off. She wouldn't let me go to the doctor. It got to the stage when I could hardly walk downstairs, and I told the family doctor; my mother hated me for it. I was in hospital two hours later.

So you have now a picture of what I've been through, and how I'm really trying to make good of life. And I wish the Council would understand how much energy that alone is taking up, without this goddamned bed-and-breakfast thing hanging over our head for the better part of two years. But the drug world . . . I smoke marijuana; and if I didn't I would crack up.

Antonia's father worked for the Mafia. We sold about fifty pounds of hashish three times a year. And we'd make a profit, three times a year, and we hardly had to lift a finger to do any work. It was very groovy. Didn't last for long, though, before this ex-bank robber came and said, 'Look, it's run out. What about this?' And he threw down a big bag of powder. I'd never seen heroin before in my life. I was 18, my husband was 36. That was it. He was off. You see he had, in the sixties, been a junkie. Then I began to realise that I couldn't put my feet up and relax unless I had a little heroin, and that was when I realised I was actually needing it. Just snorting it. He went from bad to worse and worse to terrible. He was *really* violent. On my wedding day I had bruises everywhere and I couldn't tell anyone, because I felt such an idiot. It got to the point where it was really really hell living with him. And I told him, 'If you don't get the strength to stop, you'll overdose, and you'll probably drag me down with you, you bastard.' So he'd say, 'Well I can't come off while you're here,' so I'd go away for a week and I'd come back, and rather than use the time I was away to be sick in privacy, he'd have people round. One day he got arrested. Scotland Yard set him up; he got six years. And I saw him comfortably into gaol. I was delighted, it was the best thing that could have happened. I hated him, loathed him. When he'd been in about four months I said, 'Right, Jack, that's it. I'm filing for divorce. I'm not going to sit around and wait for six years; you were an idiot and I warned you constantly. I've no conscience, I'm sorry. I'm not going to cry for you.'

I did, at one time, love him passionately. And my child from him. That's what I really wanted. I'm very glad to have made that decision. Antonia was eight months old when he left. He was pathetic with a child, he was no good. He was all right as seed but no good as a father.

On a practical level within the hotel itself, I think it would make it much better, if they put families with children in a separate hotel. Not together with the druggies, these really wraithlike men, who are just as bad as the alcoholics, and the mad people. Don't put the women and the children and the single parents and the families there. Because apart from depressing them, there's an element of danger. You have to let your six-year-old out of that room, but you know there are mad people there. The only way I could live with people like that was if I was being paid to help them. Or if I was a Mother Teresa.

Then on the other side – red tape: they've got to cut it, they've got to stop this boundary bullshit. They turn round and say, 'Jenny, your work is a very good point. You get points for working, *but*, you don't get points because you weren't working when you moved in. They say, if you stay in the area of Westminster for two years then you're automatically entitled to be housed. But if you are in a bed-and-breakfast, you are in limbo, it doesn't count as being anywhere. It's like sitting in an airport: you're on neutral zone. I want to give them money, I don't want to take anything from them.

It's such a waste of money living in the hotel, because we'd rather pay rent. It's £300 a week, of which I pay £32. If they give me a beaten-up, run-down flat I'll give them money and I'll make it beautiful. That's all I want. I know they've got properties.

I think the staff in the hotels should be chosen for a skill, or at least be mature adults. They're disreputable people, they're people with nothing up here; it's a doss of a job. I wouldn't have met you for the first time up there in the hotel. I would have been totally defenceless.

I think I would vote Conservative now. I couldn't vote for the Labour Party. I've absolutely no faith or understanding of what they're trying to do, and I don't like this union business anyway. I think it stinks. I don't think it makes any difference which government is in power. I think the housing situation is a mess. I think it's down to each individual and their capabilities, as to what actually happens to them. I do have to blame myself. I don't know that much about politics, to form too many opinions right now.

At the end of the interview, Jenny kissed me. A few days later I heard through a mutual friend that Jenny had been the victim of a violent assault. She had been beaten up and almost strangled in her hotel room, while her daughter was there. The man involved was taken into police custody.

A year later I spoke to Jenny again. After two years in bed and breakfast, she was moved to two different hotels in a month. She was so frustrated by this that she finally made a scene: she shouted at the Council and screamed that she would end up in an institution if she wasn't rehoused. Almost immediately, she was given a temporary housing association flat in W1. This flat only costs £18 a week – far cheaper, as well as far more comfortable, than her hotel room. Jenny still has her supermarket job, her daughter is at the same school and, according to her mother, is 'blooming'. Jenny still hasn't been permanently rehoused, but this footnote to her story shows that, in the case of the homeless, everything certainly doesn't come to she who waits.

PART TWO

Interviews with politicians

The two Conservative politicians interviewed here both seem to be saying, 'The market will provide, but we won't.' Theresa Gorman MP, whose faith in market forces is quite mystical, is nostalgic for the nineteenth century, when the Peabody Dwellings and other housing schemes for the poor were set up, *not* at State expense. Charities are, understandably, alarmed by the Government's expectation that they should shoulder the burden of responsibility for welfare. Downing Street has asked for a list of all voluntary groups and charities receiving public money, and many people in the voluntary sector are afraid this will restrict their campaigning activities.

Another likely development is that the Government will repeal or alter both the Immigration Act and the Homeless Persons' Act, developments which Patricia Kirwan, ex-Chair of Westminster City Council Housing Committee, is so keen to see. This would not in any way help the housing crisis but will conveniently 'disappear' many people from the homelessness statistics. It would make it possible for the Government legally to repatriate many people who have nowhere to live, and to deny responsibility for many others.

There is no love lost between Theresa Gorman and Patricia Kirwan. The latter told me that she had sacked Theresa Gorman from her post as Vice-chair of the Westminster Housing Committee after six weeks. I chose to interview these two women because they are both outspoken political mavericks who have been involved in Westminster City Council housing policies. Patricia Kirwan is a well-known local figure in Bayswater.

Jackie Rosenberg is a young Labour councillor on Westminster City Council who points out that Conservative housing policy in the area has more to do with gerrymandering than with concern for the homeless. She describes two effective campaigns: one to prevent Westminster City Council putting prefabricated houses on a wasteland site in Barking to 'house' their homeless and a second, which has not yet concluded, to enable the tenants on her estate to buy their houses from Westminster City Council at a cost *to* the Council of £30m.

Patricia Kirwan

Patricia Kirwan is a Conservative councillor in the City of Westminster and was, until June 1987, Chair of the Westminster City Council Housing Committee. In 1987 Patricia Kirwan stood against Lady Porter in the contest for Leadership of Westminster City Council, and lost. She was one of the few Conservatives to vote against selling off the Westminster cemeteries for 15p (possibly the silliest decision ever made by a Council). She is now isolated from her fellow Tories on the Council.

Patricia Kirwan is 46, married, with no children. On the telephone, when we were making arrangements to meet, she described herself with characteristic frankness: 'I'm short, fat, blonde and middle-aged.' The interview took place in an Indian restaurant, where Patricia Kirwan ate the delicious vegetarian food heartily despite her views on immigration.

Patricia Kirwan asserts that many of the homeless are 'just girls who've gone out and got pregnant'. In fact, the rate of births to young women nationally has fallen since 1971. In the South East, including London, the rate of births to young women has been even lower than this national figure. As for 'illegitimate' births, a favourite target of Conservative politicians, they tend increasingly to be to older women and registered to both parents. Generally, families with young children are a falling proportion of Britain's households (from 39 per cent in 1971 to 31 per cent in 1985). It is true that such households account for 70 per cent of those the local authorities agree to help: but this is because the law excludes most other homeless people from applying. Homelessness has increased, not because of changing social patterns but because there is a chronic shortage of low-cost rented accommodation.

Patricia Kirwan: I've always been interested in politics. I was brought up in Africa, in Kenya, during the Wind of Change and before Independence. Anyway, I came over here really not political. When I got married we bought a flat in Westbourne Terrace, and we tried to find out who our landlord was. It was just before the 1971 GLC elections. You started having a go at all the political parties, and the Conservatives said, 'If you think it's so easy, do it yourselves.' So we got involved that way, really. But my two main interests have always been housing and education. The two are so closely linked, the basis of everything. I was a GLC member for four years and lost to Ken Livingstone in 1981, and I went off to Westminster in 1982 and became Housing Chairman in 1983. They've got a four-year rule, so I came off in June 1987.

I've always lived around here, since 1964. So I do know it extremely well. And I've seen it change. A lot of it's changed for better. The housing conditions in North Paddington, for example, in the last 12 years have just totally transformed. But then there's the deterioration, as one might say, of Bayswater. I think it started with far too many hotels anyway; there was a cut in the tax in 1970 which gave £1,000 a room to hoteliers, then the cheap tourist trade grew and grew, and then came this mad rush of homeless families, and of course so many of the hoteliers saw a quick buck – more than a quick buck – and now it is absolutely unbelievable.

I represent the Lancaster Gate ward and I did actually find some figures for you. This is in a very small ward with a population of about 4,000. These are numbers of families, not people: Ealing 197, Camden 58, Haringey 106. Hammersmith and Fulham 57, Newham 52, Tower Hamlets 26. You're talking about at least 1,500 people. Then you wonder, What on earth's it for? You get terribly cynical, and you think, Aha! Marginal council, the local boroughs are trying to flood it out.

Going back 30 or 40 years, the population[1] of Westminster was something like 500,000. We're now down to about 175,000. Yet again, going back over the last 15 or 20 years, the amount of council accommodation in Westminster has gone up phenomenally. Council estate accommodation, housing association – low rent, fair rent stuff. There's not going to be much of an impact [from Westminster selling off 50 per cent of their accommodation]. So, if the population's dropped that much, the rented accommodation in the public sector has gone right up – why the problem? Why are there so many homeless coming through when in fact the amount of state housing has gone up enormously? Yet the actual residential population has dropped so much. Is it a difference in family units? Upbringing? I don't know – influxes of people coming into England? Certainly, as far as we're concerned, Westminster is the centre of the world. We've got Piccadilly Circus, train stations, everyone comes pouring in. They're homeless, we've got to take them in. Until we decide if we can trace them or not.

They're *not* local people. Then you ask yourself, should they be in hotels? In Bayswater? Or where did they come from? Why did they leave?

I am extremely sorry for Tower Hamlets. They have got a *mad* influx of Bangladeshis. There is no way that any local authority can cope with a totally false influx, because you can't plan them. Even if they were good at housing, which they're not. People are not meant to come into this country unless they can look after themselves. We wouldn't be allowed to go to India or Nigeria or Switzerland or France or anywhere else. So I think immigration policies are partly to blame for all this. And then, the Irish – they're not working. Living on the State – here's the right-wing Tory coming out in me. But it does irritate me beyond measure when I see genuine Westminster residents, or Londoners, who cannot get something, because they're being overtaken by these people who in fact are jumping the queue.

You look at what the other boroughs have got in terms of empty housing. Ealing 564, Camden 1049, Hammersmith 665, Newham . . . They're saying they haven't got the money; but they could do what we did. I sold off a certain amount of vacant properties into deals with the private sector, in order to renovate the rest. There are always ways round it. Other councils don't want to. They could.

I invented a thing called the barter system, which the Treasury couldn't fault. They were furious with me. You said to a developer, 'Right. We've got, say, a couple of tower blocks which are totally run down, full of asbestos, awful.' Say there was an estate up in North Paddington which had about 600 flats on it, of which about 30 or 40 per cent were empty. They were crumbling, they were in a dreadful state. So we said to the developer, 'Right. It's going to cost us £38m. to put this lot right, which we're not going to have for years and years. You can have the tower block and, say, 50 flats at the end of the day, in return for which you do up the rest of the properties for us.' That's exactly what we're doing. Most people on our waiting list are housed.[2] I know loads of people who are on the waiting list because one day they might want a flat. So I think waiting lists are in fact not a particularly good measure of demand, or measure of need. You see in the old days, before we got the influx of homeless families, the chances are that a young couple, say sons or daughters of council tenants, would wait two or three years and then get to the top of the waiting list and they would get something.

The women you've been talking to, where do they come from?
MM: Well, quite a few of them from London —
PK: Are many of them single women, one-parent families?

MM: I think about 70 per cent of the adults in the rooms are single families, but an awful lot of them aren't.

PK: But are they battered wives, divorcees, or are they just girls who've gone out and got pregnant?

MM: They're all kinds of different people —

PK: Because, it sounds terribly cynical, but it is the oldest trick in the book: you want to jump the queue, if you're a young girl – because it's part and parcel of their way of life. Pretend you've had a row with your parents, pretend you've got slung out, get pregnant, the Council's got to house you. And there's an awful lot of that and one wonders, you know . . .

What I think ought to happen in these cases [battered women] is that the courts ought to order possession of the family home to the mother of the children. If the husband tries to come back he should be sent to prison for contempt of court. And, frankly, if they go around beating their wives, I don't give a damn what happens to the husbands.

I tried it when I was at Westminster, I said, 'Come on, we've got to try this.' 'No, you can't risk it. These women are at risk, we're not allowed to do it.' So I said, 'Okay. Well why can't we link them up?' – I don't know if you've come across these emergency lifeline telephones? Pensioners have them – 'No. Not allowed to do it.' And this I think is absolutely stark raving mad, because it is lunacy for these women to be thrown out of their home. It's thoroughly bad for the children, because I mean a family break-up is traumatic enough for a child. So think the law needs revising.

MM: I think certainly that saying someone who escapes from a violent man is intentionally homeless is mad. I think it's a very dubious phrase anyway because nobody's actually intentionally homeless. They might do silly things, but nobody deliberately goes out and makes themself homeless. I think it's rather an offensive phrase.

PK: I think so too. A lot of these girls do.

MM: Well I haven't come across one.

PK: Obviously one is extremely worried about the children. Because it is not a way to bring up children, it's not a way to bring up the next generation. You're building up a complete sort of sub-society, aren't you? Which is dependent on the State, with terrible moral and alienation problems. The children are extremely resilient, if they get the chance. You see they really should not be in the centre of London. If they're going to be unemployed, or can't work, I really do think there are so many little towns in the North of England where you can buy properties for £5,000, £10,000. Frankly if I were a council and I could get away with it – it is better for them to be put there in the interim than living in these hotels.

Government housing policies have been such as to actually stop a reasonable privately rented accommodation market.

MM: And do you think the new Housing Act will solve that? Because there's no mention of homelessness in it.

PK: Nothing's going to solve it. But it might make it easier.

MM: Why do you think the draft for the new Act doesn't mention homelessness? Is it going to be dealt with in some other Act?

PK: No, I don't think they're going to touch homelessness. They've got the Homeless Persons' Act, I don't think they're going to change it. It says councils are responsible for housing people in their own areas. But London councils physically cannot take on people who come in from overseas, people who come in from Ireland, people who come down from Glasgow looking for work – we haven't got the land to do it. So I don't know whether the new Housing Act will help. I hope it will.

I don't think it will help in Central London. Because our land values are too high. What I'm saying is, they shouldn't be in the centre of London. Where I think the Housing Bill might help is by freeing rented accommodation outside – in areas like Ealing. Newham, for example, has got 4,400 empty properties in the private sector. Now if those could be brought back in, even if they're not particularly marvellous – We (Westminster) have got 7,000. It's a bit like the black market: where there's a shortage, which there is now, prices go up. If there's more, they'll stabilise. Up until recently, the Housing Benefit picked up most cases. I wait to see what is going to happen with the great and glorious Government's latest on that.

MM: So what's your private explanation for why the situation, over eight or nine years, has become so much worse?

PK: I just don't know. I think there's a breakdown of family life, to a certain extent. There are more divorces than ever before, more one-parent families, more unmarried mothers, so there's been, in the last 20 years, a complete change in the life-style of people. Aspirations have changed, society's got very much more open. If you're an unmarried mum now it doesn't really matter, whereas in the old days, you know, it was appalling – shock, horror. People keep their children; 30 years ago they'd have had them adopted. Unemployment in the North, and immigration. A certain amount of people being evicted by bad landlords or other landlords who want possession of the houses.

MM: And what about the Council's policy to sell off housing? Do you feel that's contributed to the problem?

PK: No, I don't think that's contributed at all. I honestly genuinely don't. But on the whole, where you're selling, your tenants will be entitled to housing anyway. Westminster's housing stock even now is 23,000. Say they sell 1,000 a year for the next four years – you're still going to be up to 19 or 20,000, which is more than was there ten years ago. I was worried about this policy, I must admit, I didn't think it was going to work. It did worry me that it would make the homelessness worse, that people wouldn't get transfers, that the only people who would buy would be people who weren't council tenants or housing association tenants or their children – and in fact that isn't happening. The people who are buying under the designated sales scheme are in fact our own tenants.[3] So they're leaving to buy something else, thereby freeing up something else for renting. So I think it's going to have a minimal effect, I don't think it's going to have a major effect. It has only been in effect for the last six or eight months. I did do a certain amount of selling off, but that was to get the money in order to do up other accommodation.

MM: Do you feel homelessness is to any extent the fault of the people it happens to?

PK: I do think, sometimes. Without them realising it. But I don't think people think like that – it's terribly easy to say, 'It is your fault, you should not have had that baby.' Or, 'You should have taken your husband to court and got possession of the house.' If you've been beaten black and blue, and a lot of them are, the last thing you want to do is stand up in court; you just want to run away and hide. So, yes it's their fault but no, it's not, if you see what I mean. I don't want to sound hard. I wish we could do far more. I think that's the type that I most feel sorry for.

I am desperately sorry for a lot of these Bangladeshis who come over here. And there are thousands and thousands of them. Tower Hamlets is going absolutely spare. These girls are Hindus, or Moslems, and were brought up in that sort of very restrictive society; the women don't know how to cope because the men are not behaving there as they would at home. I don't think they ought to come. That is not meant to sound racist, it's meant to be actually practical: it is wrong for them to come, and their children, because we simply cannot cope. And why England has got to be the only country in the whole world that takes everybody in who wants to come, is completely beyond me.

MM: So would you favour changing immigration laws?

PK: Absolutely. I would put a stop to all this immigration, if I could. Completely.

MM: Including from Ireland?

PK: Oh, absolutely.

MM: From the North of England?

PK: No, within the country, no – I think you've got to somehow get going – and the Government is trying – there has got to be more mobility. Alternatively, there has to be more job creation in the North to stop people coming down to the South East. Because it's not just the homeless family problem, it's the problem on the Green Belt. I was listening to Michael Heseltine on L B C this morning, about the Green Belt being totally destroyed, fields, new towns, etc., all in the South East; totally unnecessary. What's going to happen to Kent with the Channel Tunnel, God only knows. But I think the North is beginning to pick up. With a bit of luck there'll be less pressure on people to come down.

It isn't quite how the E E C regulations work, but I would like to say that nobody can come over here until they can prove that they a) have a job and b) have the wherewithal to house themselves without calling on the State. But do they need to live in the centre of London? Where are the jobs?

MM: Well actually a lot of these people do have jobs in the centre, and they would lose those jobs if they were suddenly moved to some small town way outside. There are more jobs around London.

PK: Somehow you've got to get these empty properties owned by the councils and the private sector into use. I don't like the Government's centralisation at the moment. It worries me the way they're going against local government. But I can understand why they're trying to set up Housing Action Trusts and things like this, separately, to try to cope. I would love to get my mitts on Tower Hamlets or Haringey or Newham's housing and do something about it. I reckon within three years I could get at least half that lot into use as fair-rented property, and that would solve a hell of a problem.

MM: Then why do so many councils say that they can't do it? That precisely the Government policy is stopping them?

PK: Because they haven't got the imagination to get round it, and they don't really, in their heart of hearts, want to get rid of the municipal housing estates. They like them. Because for a Labour councillor it is power. The council estates do represent power. When you have total control over people's lives, through their rents, through their housing, whatever, you can make damned sure they vote for you. Keeps you there. You give people freedom, you do it up – I've now seen this again and again – you sort out their problems on a housing estate, and they don't vote Labour like mad. But they always have done until then.

MM: People in the hotels do not vote. They're almost disenfranchised, effectively if not actually. They can't even get a GP. So they're like non-citizens, this is the sinister thing.

PK: I do agree with Richard Stone on this – the health problems in these hotels do need special treatment, they really do.[4]

MM: They're dreadful! If the environmental health officers come round, how come practically everybody I've spoken to has had a room infested with cockroaches?

PK: There is a limit to what one can do with resources which are finite.[5]

MM: As a council, does Westminster have any control over the situation in hotels?

PK: Very little. We try, with Social Services, to pick up some of them. We tried to get a code of conduct through the various boroughs when I was chairman; about where they put the homeless; that they let us know that they will provide Social Service back-up. And that they would pay us to do environmental health checks. We're having to check up on around about 100 hotels.[6]

They [people in the hotels] are getting more alienated, because their children behave appallingly badly. The level of vagrancy and drunkenness and children begging is appalling. That creates alienation from the local community, who are up in arms. In my particular ward, they've just about had it, and so have the shopkeepers. It is reaching cracking point. I don't think the Government does realise the scale of the problem. I've had goes at them about it over the years.

MM: Who have you approached? It puzzles me where the buck does stop. If William Waldegrave [then Housing Minister, who attended a recent public meeting in Bayswater] didn't appear to be very aware of what was going on, who is?

PK: He is damn well aware of what's going on. He's been told, again and again and again. I think they don't know what the answer is. I wasn't at the meeting with Waldegrave. I'm sure he looked terribly caring and concerned.

MM: Well, he looked surprised as well, when he was told that in the hotel next to where the toy library is, there are some families paying £1,000 a week for one room. Now that is economic insanity. Even if some ministers might not care about anything else, surely they care about money! And after all, it's somebody's money.

PK: It all comes down to the fact that, at the moment, everybody thinks in terms of Bayswater, and I'm saying, 'No, we literally haven't got the room.'

MM: Could you simply close down the hotels?

PK: No. We closed one down, called the Sandringham, and we closed another one too. We do have goes at them the whole time. But of course the thing changes so often, you see. You get your person [inspector] in, they have a blitz through the hotel, take them to court, things get better for six months, and then they go downhill again.

MM: They have an awful lot of power, the people who are managing the hotels, and they've got no qualifications, as far as I can see.

PK: No, they haven't. There should be far more back-up from the boroughs who put their families here. Frankly each borough ought to have a permanent Social Services team. We would love to get hold of some of these hotels – close them down, buy them and turn them into residential property. Can't do it. Planning law. Once you've got planning permission —

MM: And you can't withdraw that licence as you can, say, from a restaurant?

PK: No. It's not a licence. You can take them to court, you can fine them. We would *love* to get rid of half these hotels round here.

What you do find with the homeless families is that an awful lot of people just disappear. You don't know where they've gone, they've made alternative arrangements – something like 30 or 40 per cent of the people who come to us. I'm not saying Westminster doesn't have a problem, we've got a hell of a problem. But I like to think that we handle it better. It's only very recently that we've started looking outside the area, to put people.

MM: Well where are you putting them now?

PK: I don't know – I think you'll find, a hotel in Croydon somewhere. They're looking at these rather glamorous temporary houses now, we were trying to find empty land to put those on, because they're rather good.

MM: You mean Nissen huts?

PK: No, no! Not Nissen! Prefab. But the modern sort. We couldn't find the land and get planning permission to put those up. We were trying. Take Westminster; if we were only responsible for Westminster-type people, we could cope. But because the legislation is so very widely drawn, anybody can come to us and we have to put them up somewhere while we're investigating them. That's why we use hotels. Very few people from Westminster are in hotels for longer than six months.

MM: Is there any move to stop giving planning permission to hotels?

PK: We stopped giving planning permission a very long time ago. Ten, fifteen years. But the damage had been done by then, there were so many of them.

The only thing you can hope for, I think, is that the homeless families thing somehow dries up: they stop making as much money, so they sell them to somebody who wants to turn them into flats or homes. If, suddenly, all these people were to move out of Westminster, there would be an awful lot of empty hotels, which tourists wouldn't want to know. They might make more money out of them converting them back to residential. They'd certainly get planning permission for that, extremely fast. I don't like to see the population of my ward and the Bayswater area, the residential population, going down as fast as it is. It's wrong. It is soon going to be only the very rich and the very poor. We've recently done a survey of the people who are leaving, and they are people – late thirties, forties, early fifties – who don't want their children to go to the local schools; they can afford to move, so they're going.

MM: Will you stay here, do you think?

PK: No. We've bought a cottage out in Gloucestershire, and as soon as my husband retires we'll be out. No – oh dear, this is a terrible thing to say – I'm still fond of the area, obviously, otherwise I'd go and live somewhere else in London. But I don't like the dirt, I don't like the squalor, I don't like the social pressures. Perhaps I'm just getting old. Who was it who said, once you are tired of London you are tired of life? But it's expensive and it's dirty and it's messy.

MM: Do you feel that Central Government understands the situation?

PK: No. I think what they've said is, 'we have passed legislation which says homeless families have to be housed; we've done what we can, it's up to the local authorities now'. So they're blaming it on the councils. I did go to the Home Office on a couple of occasions on the immigration thing, and they said, 'People can't come into the country unless they can prove they've got somewhere to live.' I said, 'But they're patently not. You've got to do something.' The Home Office was furious with me. During my time as Housing Chairman I spoke to every Secretary of State and Minister that ever existed. And we've been through a fair number of them. I have been as far as advisers at Number Ten Downing Street. And I know that Shirley Porter has discussed the matter with the Prime Minister. You can't go much higher than that.

MM: And do you know what kind of response she got?

PK: 'Tut, tut, oh yes what a terrible, dreadful world, we'll see what we can do about it.'

MM: What about other politicians? Any sort of hint that some of them do know what's going on, and do care, and have any ideas what could be done? Or do you feel it's only local politicians who have any grasp of the situation?

PK: I don't know. I think if you're a minister it's terribly easy to get caught up in an ivory tower at the Department of the Environment, and look at statistics. Statistics, really, can be made to prove everything or nothing. The Government will say exactly what I've done: 'Look, there are all these empty properties, get them all into use.' You can get them into use, if you're prepared to go along with private sector development and involvement of private money; it can be done. But a lot of the Labour boroughs do not have the political will to do it, because they don't want to get shot of their housing.

MM: But what the Labour boroughs are saying is that they can't do it because Central Government make it impossible for them to re-use the money that they're getting from selling off the council houses.

PK: It is possible.

MM: And do you think Central Government would turn a blind eye to it if they did?

PK: Well, they did with me. There are ways round it. And I think, in a way, Tower Hamlets are beginning to try. But of course they're under Liberal control now. At the last count, they've got 3,500 empty properties. A lot of them might be in tower blocks. Some of them are unsuitable for families, some of them not. But you can certainly convert tower blocks to extremely good sheltered accommodation for elderly people. If you put in the right sort of lifts and you have a concierge downstairs and you do them up nicely. Absolutely ideal.

We will have brought back a thousand renovated dwellings, which wouldn't have been available otherwise. So – we will have lost a certain amount of housing stock, but we'll have super modern flats and places to put people in. And that could be done. But it is on the whole the loony lefty boroughs, isn't it, who've got the worst problem? And the incompetent ones. And they are very, very, very incompetent. I mean Hackney's very incompetent. Tower Hamlets has been appallingly incompetent for years.

I horrified the Conservative old ladies a couple of years ago by saying, 'You know, when I first came to live round here in 1964, you could find somewhere to rent. Nowadays if I were that age I'd probably be squatting.' You could see the horror on the old ladies' faces. It's rather fun, isn't it? But I mean it!

But I do wish these girls would think twice before getting pregnant and running away from home. It's not fair on the others and it's not fair on them and it's not fair on their children. And so many – in the trade I think they're called parental chuck-outs. In my generation you stayed at home until you could sort yourself out, you shared flats, did things like that.

MM: Housing policy has to follow these trends, rather than try to turn them backwards.

PK: I wonder whether the trends will reverse themselves. I think A I D S might help.

In many European countries, low-cost housing is not provided simply by the State, but an awful lot of money is put in by pension funds, insurance companies and so forth. I think people are going to have to be prepared to pay more for housing themselves.

It is awful, isn't it, that there is more prosperity in this country than there has ever been, in real terms? And yet the pockets of deprivation are getting worse.

MM: Would you agree that the rich really have got richer and the poor have got poorer in the last ten years?

PK: No. I think more of the poor have now got richer.

Notes

1 In 1951 the population of Westminster, according to the Census, was 300,000. By 1981 this had declined to 191,000. However, the two figures were differently calculated; in the earlier census, everybody sleeping in the area that night was counted. The population of Westminster reached the figure of half a million which Patricia Kirwan mentions as long ago as 1851.

2 As Mary Tester's interview shows, Westminster's interpretation of what is genuine homelessness is such that few people manage to get on to the waiting list.

3 In order to qualify under Westminster's designated sales policy, applicants must be first-time buyers, and fit into one of the following categories: (a) a Westminster City Council tenant; (b) a tenant of a housing association in Westminster where the housing association agrees to take a nominated tenant in return; (c) homeless persons or families Westminster are responsible for, or Westminster housing waiting-list applicants (in May 1989 there 9,000 on the waiting list); (d) people who have worked continuously in Westminster for three years.

4 Richard Stone is a local G P, and co-chair of the Bayswater Project.

5 Patricia Kirwan told me that all the hotels used by Westminster are inspected once a month by environmental health inspectors. The ones used by other boroughs are inspected every three months.

6 See Jackie Rosenberg's comments on this code, pp.123–38.

Theresa Gorman

Theresa Gorman has been Conservative MP for Billericay since June 1987, and was previously a Westminster councillor for four years. I decided to interview her because she is a prominent and eccentric Conservative politician who has been involved in Westminster housing policies. I arranged to meet her by letter, and printed at the foot of her reply on House of Commons writing paper was the maxim: *'The State is the great fiction by which everyone seeks to live at the expense of everyone else.' Frederick Bastiat 1801–1850.*

We met one afternoon in the crowded Central Lobby of the House of Commons, and while I was waiting for her a curious ritual involving the Mace was acted out. There was a cry of 'Speaker!', with an oddly juvenile intonation, like a child announcing 'Coming!' in a game of hide-and-seek. The crowd parted to admit an immensely solemn procession of men dressed in anachronistically formal clothes. One was bewigged, another clutched the Mace (this was just a few days before Ron Brown disgraced himself with it), at the same angle as a little boy marching with a gun. Then there was a cry of 'Hats Off!' Two policemen obediently removed their helmets. Nobody else in the Easter crowd was wearing a hat, but a few tourists tittered, not sure whether this was British Heritage or British Humour.

Theresa Gorman is 56, with grey hair and a nervous expression. She led me through the basement labyrinth of seedy canteens until we sat over coffee in a remote, shabby dining room. I thought how peculiarly English it was to have all that splendour upstairs and squalor downstairs.

True to type as a professional politician, Theresa Gorman is difficult to interrupt. My attempts to begin a more intimate dialogue met with genteel but firm hostility. Her manner is absolutely self-assured, impatient and righteous. She has a tendency to frown, to wrinkle her nose disdainfully and to purse her lips, as she discusses the many topics that irritate her.

Theresa Gorman: Loads and loads of people come into Westminster for accommodation. We mostly put them on a train if they came from Birmingham or wherever, and sent them back home. But a lot of other boroughs, like Brent, would use the hostels or rather the little hotels for their bed-and-breakfast people. Some councils, Brent, or Camden, Islington, have what you'd call a reputation for accommodating anybody that turns up. Whereas other boroughs, like Hounslow – I think because of their proximity to London Airport – and us in Westminster, have to be considerably more circumspect. Otherwise we'd have three-quarters of the population from other parts of the world, and all the country, because I mean everybody wants to live in the centre of London. So we are the prime site for that sort of problem.

MM: What do you think of using bed-and-breakfast accommodation as any kind of temporary or permanent solution to homelessness?

TG: Well, I personally would have repealed the Homeless Persons' Act, because I think to some extent it has stimulated a lot of the problem. I believe that a lot of legislation is counter-productive, and I think that's one example. I don't know whether Patricia Kirwan said that, but the general feeling on Westminster City Council was that we would like the act repealed. Homelessness isn't a problem except in inner cities, I think. Well the problem, of course, is entirely produced by the Rent Acts. If we didn't have the Rent Acts, hundreds of thousands of ordinary people would let rooms or part of their houses. We identified, I think, in Westminster over 10,000 units of accommodation which were kept out of use. You know, areas where people had flats which were half rates[1] because they wouldn't let them, or rather would only let them to holiday lets. So the Rent Act completely distorts the use of property, coupled with the fact that lots of local councils within the catchment area of London – like Peckham, Southwark – have loads of flats in council blocks which are out of use. Maybe vandalism, but very often just mismanagement of the housing department. And, you know, there are these exchange schemes and really they were set up in order to make use of some of the outlying property.[2] But it's never really worked. So many people who come into the city won't go outside it for accommodation. They won't go to Southwark. They won't cross the river. They want to be in the centre of London. And the Act doesn't allow you to actually make them go where there is a flat within reasonable travelling distance. Well, it gives you, I think, statutory powers to do quite a lot. I sat on numerous tribunals of dispute over this, where people were being asked to go somewhere else and wouldn't go there even though there was accommodation, even just as far as Peckham, which isn't exactly the ends of the earth. On the other hand, outer boroughs don't want to take too many of your so-called homeless people because they don't want to get loaded with what they regard as problem families, or individuals.

There is this report from the States, the Institute for Economic Affairs are going to publish it, and the correlation between what they call the bag-lady syndrome and the degree of control of the rent in the area concerned is amazing. I lived in New York for two years and exactly the same problem exists there: they are heavily into rent control of the older properties, very few people will build anything to let except very luxurious blocks of flats for high rentals, and those people that have got accommodation to let outside the Rent Acts can charge what they like for it. Which is exactly what happens in London. So you get asked £175 for what's just basically a bedsitting room, you know, in the centre. It's ridiculous that people can charge that!

MM: But what's even more ludicrous is the prices that are being paid for the rooms in the bed-and-breakfast hotels. Some families are paying £1,000 a week for one room, and then living in squalor.

TG: I know, it's absolutely obscene. It's typical, though, of governments – any government – that once they've put an Act into place, however bad it is in its working, there is complete reluctance to do anything about it. They'd rather spend money just as a stopgap measure, like that. The whole business of Housing Benefits has grown out of the Government's reluctance to repeal the Rent Acts. They are terrified of the backlash, in terms of votes, from people who are in rent-controlled property. Because everyone says, 'Oh, if you take the controls off, the rent will go through the roof and I'll be thrown out into the street.' But that's not what happens. You can still give security of tenure for the existing tenants, at least to see them out. But all new property development has to be decontrolled. And that's still not coming in.

MM: But that would still, surely, result in a lot of homelessness, because you'd still get a lot of people who couldn't afford the rents.

TG: No, because once you've got competition coming into the market – well, there'd have to be other changes, particularly in planning. Local authorities and the nationalised services, particularly the National Health Service, are the biggest culprits of all at sitting on land and sites which could be redeveloped. Within my patch in Westminster there are three or four large nurses' hostels which had been empty for three years, while I was a councillor, and are still standing empty now. Those could be offered for rent, they could have been sold off to the private sector and converted. You can sell them with the proviso that they are used for affordable housing, or whatever. But the only way to overcome this problem is to increase the supply. And the only way you can increase the supply is for the government to make it attractive for the private sector to come in and do something about it.

In the Budget Nigel Lawson introduced the idea that you get tax concessions. You can now invest that kind of money into properties for converting for rent. It isn't true that the big institutions like insurance companies, unit trusts, do invest in [domestic] property. They invest massively in commercial property. Why? Because the money that they put in shows a reasonable return. And they would do the same, if they could, with rented property, for domestic use. The incentive isn't there. One, they have to pay through the nose at the moment because there's a shortage of such properties. If the government were to make local authorities release the land which they're sitting on – even within the centre of Westminster there's about 5,000 acres, it's reckoned[3] – if you go round London and multiply these sites, you will find masses of wasteland. The figures are not mine, they come from a publication which the Adam Smith Institute did, called *Why Waste Land?* All authorities who had more than one square mile of waste land were listed, and it's astonishing!

MM: It's very odd that in the draft of the Housing Act, homelessness isn't mentioned. Many people are homeless and working. You can have a low wage, or £10,000 a year, which is the average salary, and you still couldn't get a mortgage anywhere in London. And if your job's in London you can't just move out.

TG: Most people – young people – too, don't want a mortgage. They just want somewhere to rent. But you see, the Government could make local authorities release those sites to be sold and have written into the contract that they must be used for low-cost housing. But you see, in the past, organisations like Guinness Trust and Peabody were set up specifically for that purpose. They built these low-cost dwellings and they restricted them to people on low incomes. There's no reason why we can't replicate that all over again. Similar trusts, which I suppose the housing associations are already.

MM: Why are they selling off so much council property? Westminster are selling off 50 per cent.

TG: Once you've got people in who are there for life, those properties and the capital locked up in them are really no longer available to you. If you can sell even a whole estate to an organisation as a long-term investment on terms which will protect the tenancies, then the capital which you release by doing that you can then use for other developments. There is a catch-22 put in, because at the moment the Government only allows an authority to spend up to 20 per cent of the money it realises that way [on building]. That needs to be changed. You can use it for paying off the local authority debt.

My point really is this: anybody can be paper rich with vast amounts of property, which is what councils are. But they are in fact money poor, because the money is tied up in those sites. The authority can sell and then lease back, which is a device quite commonly used in industry. Westminster City Council doesn't own the building that it functions from. It rents. And Conservative Central Office, which bought its building, then sold it and leased it back. This way it liberated several million pounds of capital. You and I can do that – if we owned our house outright, we can remortgage. You still have the right to go on living there but the capital is released. Local authorities are paper rich.

The Labour authorities, who are by government criteria overspending, had started to do this. They'd been selling off and then leasing back their schools, which is actually very sound business practice. The Government didn't like it, because they were then using that money to carry out projects over and above their rate capitation. But nevertheless the principle, in my opinion, is right: local authorities, particularly within London, have the potential of raising masses of money.

The big City companies, who take a long-term view of these things, will, just like the nineteenth-century landowners, lease back the land at low rents. They then know that in 60 years' time that land falls into them again. In the short-term, meaning 20, 30, 40 years, local authorities have access to very large reservoirs of cash. You then have to persuade the Government to allow them to use more of it; if you earmark it specifically for housing then I think that's reasonable. If, as in the past, the authorities have then gone off and done things which the government of the day thinks to be daft, or inappropriate – we needn't have a debate about what that is – then you do have problems.

But the principle is right: if I were Housing Leader on Westminster City Council, which I never was – it's a pity in a way because I'd have done a lot more imaginative things. We're recording this but Patricia Kirwan and I didn't always see eye to eye. I felt that Westminster Council had the opportunity to do really interesting things which could have been emulated by other parts of the country. But in fact I don't think we did do very much, not a fraction of what we could have done.

I would have taken blocks which were hard to let, unattractive – we do have some, even in Westminster – and sold them to the private sector; just got rid of them and used that money. We had for example, in the North Westminster area, several tower blocks. They'd got asbestos in them and people hated living in them. Had there been a gas accident like Ronan Point in them we would have emptied them out like a shot. We would have got them clear and then we would have flogged them off.

In my particular ward, we have a dreadful estate; Page Street Estate, immediately behind Westminster Hospital, reckoned to be one of the worst estates in London. What's called colloquially a 'sink' estate. Nobody who was living there wanted to stay; 90 per cent of my surgery was people from Page Street saying, 'Can you get me out.' Yet it was a prime site! It abutted on to two of the most expensive blocks of flats in London – Marsham Court and Westminster Gardens. Any one of those blocks, we could have sold for an *enormous* sum of money. Do what Dolphin Square does. They took one of their blocks and they did it up and they let it for holiday lets. The money they make out of that one block allows them to run the rest of Dolphin Square at peppercorn rents. We could do the same kind of thing. We are in a key position to raise money. If I'd've been Chair of Westminster, I'd've badgered the Government to badger the Health Service to let us have some of those nurses' homes which they've been sitting on. The Health Service has had no real incentive, until recent times, to sell off all this.

MM: St Mary's, Paddington are selling off —

TG: Are they? Well about time too.

MM: Well it's a tragedy, really, because a lot of the low-paid catering workers and cleaners had tied jobs, which meant they had accommodation cheap which was owned by the hospital. They're now threatened with eviction by their own landlord, who is also their employer – the hospital.

TG: Well, they're very unimaginative. You can sell a building with security for your existing tenants. That is a combination of poor politics and poor management. The Government, if it really looked seriously at the need for some low-cost accommodation could say you sell a site with the proviso that you provide a certain amount of low-cost housing within that development.

On that basis you let them have sites, like the land adjoining Marylebone Station, to develop in that way. These flats are to be let in perpetuity to – well, in the past they would use things like, 'Families of the *worthy* working classes'. In today's terminology, you'd turn that into some kind of a statement or other.

MM: Why do you think Central Government are so uninterested in all this?

TG: As a political issue, it's strongly identified with the Left, unfortunately. So Shelter and people like that are always knocking the Government and saying, 'You must spend more Government money on providing council housing.' The Government doesn't want to do that because that, to the Government, is expanding the captive vote of the Labour Party. I mean, that's absolutely the truth. Council estates almost invariably return Labour candidates. By being political and partisan, I feel, organisations like Shelter have to some extent defeated their own object. While there was lashings of money and all parties were pursuing similar socialist lines, including the Tory Party, everything went on hunkydory. Now the Government sees putting money into council development as a way of just rebuilding or bolstering the Labour vote.

MM: Particularly in London?

TG: Particularly in London. Most of the MPs in the inner cities are still Socialists. So the Government says to itself, in political terms, 'Why bother?' Would you? You're not in the business – *but*, if *Shelter* were to become what I call market-orientated, and went for some of these more imaginative schemes, and chivied the Government, as I do, to make local authorities produce a register of all their derelict land, and then give them six months to get rid of it – auction it off – *then* they would have an entirely different response to what they are trying to do. Ask for more Government spending and you're wasting your time.

MM: But they're spending a fortune on bed and breakfast—

TG: Well I know, and they would like to see a way out of it. But politics is a funny old business. I mean don't think that lots of good imaginative ideas come out of Central Government: they never do. The Government is concerned with the status quo. The good ideas, or bad, come from the pressure lobbies. I mean look at the Alton Bill. *Huge* pressure to bring that bill in, *huge* pressure to get it through – if 90 per cent of the females in this country were opposed it wouldn't make much difference. If Shelter and similar bodies want to get the Government on their side on homelessness, they should start looking at free-market solutions to the problem. But they are blinkered. They are run by people, who are often perfectly worthy, doctrinaire Socialists. They believe the only solution to a problem is the State. They're dealing now with a government that believes the solution to problems must be from the market: so that people like Shelter and the housing associations have got to change their act. They've got to sing a different song. If they start badgering the Government, if Shelter uses its resources to find out – for example, this was in the papers the other day. John Moore has now had a survey done which says that the N H S are sitting on 14,000 acres of marketable land and property which they're not using.

MM: Hospitals which had to be closed, because of cuts?

TG: Well, some. Or [because of] demographic changes. There are lots of hospitals which are surplus to requirements because new hospitals have been built. The point is, you've got to target where there are opportunities for development. You've got to cite good examples from the past, like the Peabodies and the Guinness Trust, who did a very good job in their day and still do.

Those are independent trusts. They don't come to the Government for money, they were given plots of land, initially, at very low prices by benevolent landowners. You may say they're not benevolent – that doesn't matter. People like the Duke of Westminster, Westminster Abbey in its day, donated sites to people like the Salvation Army and the Church Army to build hostels here. That situation could be emulated today.

MM: What do you think of Westminster Council's scheme to get hold of wasteland sites – they've tried to get permission in Barking and various other places and had it refused – and put Nissen huts, prefab houses on them?

TG: I think that's horrible, I really do. Look: one, you have to liberate the property which is available. That will take the pressure out of the market. I'm not saying that people with a room to let are going to take in a homeless family. What they will do is make their spare floor, couple of rooms, available to young people at fairly modest rents. Because the more that comes into the market, the more the rents will drop. If you get a glut coming into the market the price goes down, whether it's tomatoes or whether it's rooms to let. People that can now charge £200 a week for a grotty old dump in Bayswater will no longer be able to get that. This will take the pressure off the grottier end of the market. Some of that property can then come back in. People like Guinness Trust who now have queues of very respectable people waiting, will find a lot of that pressure taken off. They will start taking in more of what I would call the people for whom they were originally set up. New trusts can be set up.

You have to remember that in London in the late thirties, if you were an ordinary working-class family, you had a choice of housing in the private sector. There was no shortage because there were no restrictions – that's not true, there was rent control. An ordinary family, if they didn't like where they were living, could find somewhere else. Since the war, because of all the bomb damage I suppose, we went into council housing in a big way. That took away the low-cost market.

If the Government suddenly started to supply cheap cotton knickers, you would find that Marks and Spencers would no longer find it viable to sell them. That's what's happened to the housing market. Whenever the government moves in on a market, it distorts the market. As public housing grew and the private sector began to decline, then you began to

117

get more pressure on what private housing was left. Rents start going up, Government intervenes with all sorts of rent controls, and then the whole thing is completely messed up, until we clear the slate by saying, if nothing else, that all new property is totally outside rent control, and only subject to private contract. So I can let my flat to you for a month or a year. You and I agree to that, and at the end of that period if I want my flat back, you have to accept that you're going to have to change. As soon as you get that, people feel more comfortable about letting.

While there's an 'iffy or butty' situation about who's going to be the next government, it wouldn't be as successful as all that. If people felt that the next government was going to be Labour they would say, 'Well, we're not going to take a chance on sticking up a block of flats if we're going to get the Labour Party in.' But nowadays that isn't quite the same. People at the moment are fairly comfortable that the Tories are in there for quite a session. I believe that to be the case, in market terms. So I think the Government would do more imaginative things – and they will do, *if* they are being pressed.

MM: The problem is that homeless people are not organised, they're not really a lobby.

TG: Well, they're seen as Labour voters.

MM: Most of them aren't even registered to vote. It's so difficult for you, if you're being shoved around to different places at 24 hours' notice, you feel very alienated, you may or may not have a job, but you certainly don't identify – they're an astonishingly apolitical group of people.

TG: Well there is SHAC. And SHAG, is that another one?

MM: Aren't you surprised by the variety of people who end up homeless these days?

TG: I don't know a lot about the people. I do know that, having sat on tribunals, many of those whom I personally witnessed were those who had come down to London in the hopes of finding a job, lived in the centre, surrounded by jobs, and yet appeared unable to find work. Myself, I doubted some of the cases as being really genuine. I'm not denying that there are people who are homeless. I talked to the people who run the housing associations: they told me that their biggest demand now are single girls with a baby. We all know the stories which say, if you go to the town hall and ask for a flat, they'll say, 'We can't give you it unless you have a baby, and then we would give you points and you would get a flat.' A certain amount of that must go on.

I know middle-class parents, fed up with their kids at home and the stereo, who literally kick them out, with the view that the Council will have to rehouse them because they're homeless. If you took out all those categories of people – I'm not suggesting that they don't get up to all these japes *because* they can't get it any other way. But in a way what I'm saying is that bad law, which I regard as the housing Acts, create all these distorted and artificial situations.

Most homeless families may be living in a terrible room but they'll have a television and other things to go with it. The point is that the market, if there is a demand for low-cost housing, will meet that demand, just as Marks and Spencers or C & As or Woolworths provides cheap knickers. If it is allowed to do so freely: that is to say, by investing in that market it can see a reasonable return on its capital. But if you said to Marks and Spencers, you can provide underclothes for people but you're not allowed to make a profit on it, there wouldn't be a Marks and Spencers.

MM: But do you see it entirely in those terms? What about all the different categories of people who are ending up in bed and breakfast – the Bangladeshi families —?

TG: Wherever you've got a society accepting immigrants into it, you're bound to get an element of what we would consider overcrowding, which might lead to homelessness. There's a very good book, it's the history of the East End, which describes the waves of people that have come in. And you could write exactly the same story for now, with the Bangladeshis. I am sorry that the Rent Acts meant that those kind of families are not wanted in normal properties, and I'm equally sorry that local authorities have constructed their housing policies so stupidly that they get people stuck into a three-bedroom house and can't move them out! If we as Westminster were functioning as a commercial-type landlord, we should be able to say, this place has three bedrooms and this place is £40 a week, and you're going to pay the £40. I mean people don't care: if their rent is £50 a week, and we put the rent up, they don't mind if they can get Housing Benefit to pay that. There are no normal market incentives to use your money sensibly, or to use space sensibly. But if you're paying a rate for what you're using, then you respond by adapting your needs.

MM: What do you think about the people who are living in bed and breakfast now?

TG: Well – I feel sorry for them. Anybody would. You wouldn't get anybody to say that they don't feel sorry for them in these conditions. It's appalling. It's ridiculous that we are keeping bad landlords in the state of comfort which they do not deserve. The solution to that is to get more properties into the market. You will not do that unless you get the private sector to help, and unless you make it comfortable for people to freely let their property and get it back if they feel they want it. It doesn't mean uncontrolled rights for landlords to throw people out into the streets, any more than you have uncontrolled rights for people to sell you a washing machine that doesn't work – there are common laws which would protect you in those circumstances. And until you realise that property and housing is only another form of market, you will not solve this problem.

The market is geared to mass-producing anything, and the people who use the service are also the people who work in the service – I mean, hospitals have got a vested interest in low-cost housing because they need low-cost workers. To create a situation which so distorts things that they are selling off properties for their own workers is ridiculous!

MM: But they're having to because of cuts. It's either that or close down wards.

TG: Well that depends. You have to look very carefully into the budgeting of some of these health authorities to find out who it is going to. Until you go into them in detail, it's impossible – in my constituency [Billericay] we get the constant threat of the closing of the wards; when you look into it, you find we need £60,000 or £100,000 a year to keep it open. What we've found is, the hospital owns land which is worth billions. There is a source there, of money. They wouldn't have bothered to do that unless they were under pressure. I'm not saying every hospital has something like that up its sleeve, but I would have thought that the site alone of St Mary's must be worth an arm and a leg.

Sometimes people do things because they're stupid or they're just ignorant, they don't understand what opportunities there would be for them. You have to realise that the Health Service employs, per capita, fewer accountants than any other industry. There was a time, until recently, when they didn't employ accountants at all, because they didn't have to worry about these kind of decisions. The money came in, they just had to account for it, and that's how life was lived in the Health Service.

A large population, because it's a mass market, should be easier to solve, not more difficult. A mass of people actually provides you with a better incentive. If you've got a lot of people to sell to, whether it's housing or anything else, that's a bigger stimulus than a little market.

MM: So what's your prediction about bed and breakfast? Do you think it'll go on being used much longer as a solution?

TG: I'm going to say today that I hope Mrs Thatcher takes up Mother Teresa's plea for the homeless, by asking the Secretary of State to repeal the Rent Acts and so encourage the private individual to let their accommodation freely, *and* encourage the private sector to develop more low-cost housing for rent. That is the way to go about it, with this government.

The private sector provides people with what they want. Whether that's ten varieties of breakfast cereal or, you know, 44,000 different coloured skirts and sets of underwear. If you allow that same set of principles, or markets, to apply, it will provide for housing needs. The State is quite clearly incapable of doing it. With all the money we've spent over the years on housing, all we've managed to do is to provide a lot of rather unattractive council estates where many people would rather not live if they could. Ghastly tower blocks which everybody says are horrible now. The places where people like to live are the little builders' estates built between the wars – this is the irony. Everything that the Labour people on Westminster [City Council] wanted to preserve were buildings and places that were put up by the private sector before planning controls were so tight. Everything which they deplored, and I deplored, was built up under tight planning control, and by ourselves in the local authorities. So I mean, what more proof do you want of the inadequacy of the system? We tried the other way, and it hasn't worked. We have to release more land, we have to relax planning, we have to force lazy councils and others to sell the sites they've got and get private capital – I don't mean you and me, little tuppenny ha'penny bits – but I mean people like pension funds, which are awash with money – to start putting money into these developments.

MM: So you don't feel this government has made mistakes in its housing policy? Certainly, all I see is more and more beggars on the streets of London, I mean women and children begging, which you did not see a few years ago.

TG: Terrible! You can't make the poor rich by making the rich poor. You know that's an old sophism, but it's true. You have to encourage people to create wealth, because otherwise we're all poor. What has caused the homeless problem is State intervention. What's caused, to some extent, joblessness, in many parts, is that the State, for donkey's years, propped up industries that had really gone past their sell-by date. Mines and steel and all of that. And councils like Westminster, who were Conservative and should have gone in for much more imaginative policies, tend to sit on their haunches because councillors quite like the authority which goes with running the housing empire.

Funnily enough a lot of the most imaginative developments that I know about are done by Labour councils, in desperation, rather than Tory councils, who should know better.

MM: You don't think it's because they might be more in touch with the needs of people at the bottom?

TG: I think they're often more short. Having overspent and been ratecapped, they have to thrash around for ways for dealing with immediate problems, like half-derelict estates. And one way of dealing with it is to sell the damned thing off, but with certain built-in protections for the existing citizenry. So I don't care who does it; I deplore the fact that Tory councils have not made better use of the opportunities they had. Particularly in Westminster. I often did vote in a minority of one, on issues.

I don't think there's any quick solution. It's got to come through basic legislation, and there isn't the pressure in this place, yet, to repeal. Very few people here can grasp the idea that the only way to give people real security, particularly for new people who want property, is to liberate the market. That idea isn't what I would call 'top of the pops' in this place yet.

Notes

1 If a flat is uninhabited, the owner pays reduced rates, under the old rating system.
2 Hard-to-Let schemes were popular with London councils in the 1970s, but have faded out over the last seven years or so as the housing crisis has intensified.
3 This is a wild overestimation. Hyde Park and Kensington Gardens together have an area of only 635 acres. Westminster City Council owns about one-third of an acre of empty land. According to the Directory of opportunity sites in Westminster kept by the City Council, there are about 37 acres of vacant land in the area, none of which is currently owned by the local authority. In March 1989 21 per cent of vacant land was under construction. The largest site (over ten acres) was Paddington Goods Yard, formerly owned by British Rail, now owned by a private company.

Jackie Rosenberg

Jackie Rosenberg is 28. She became a Westminster Labour councillor in 1986. She has worked for a housing association and a job centre, but is not working at the moment. She has a sixteen-month-old son and, when I interviewed her, was six months pregnant. I interviewed her in her council house, on the estate in Kilburn where, as she explains in the interview, tenants are trying to buy the properties they live in and are demanding a 'dowry' from Westminster Council of £30m. Her windows, and those of neighbouring houses, are plastered with signs telling developers to keep out. Her husband is the co-ordinator of the action group carrying out this imaginative campaign.

At the end of the interview, when I asked her if she had any further political ambitions, Jackie Rosenberg replied that she wanted to continue to serve as a councillor for at least a few more years. Recent legislation has made it impossible to serve one authority (i.e. as a councillor) and work for another if you earn more than £13,000 a year. This new rule has scotched any career she might have had in local government, so she plans to retrain when her children are school age.

I wanted to find a local Labour politician who would provide a counterbalance to what Patricia Kirwan and Theresa Gorman have to say. Jackie Rosenberg argues that Conservative housing policies are discriminatory and callous, and that Westminster City Council is far more concerned with shipping in 'desirable' Conservative voters than with helping the homeless. The fact that there is a Conservative majority of only four on the Council makes this particularly relevant.

Jackie Rosenberg: Westminster Council, far from ignoring issues of homelessness, is actually generating its own homeless problem by the policies it is pursuing at the moment. The Council operates a Building A Stable Community policy which means 50 per cent of all council accommodation in Westminster, as it becomes available and vacant, is being boarded up with steel doors and sold to buyers who have the cash

123

to pay for it. Consequently, of course, the Council has admitted, its costs for homelessness are going to have to rise proportionately, because they know that they are thus reducing the available accommodation for homeless people. They are also generating a whole new layer of homeless people who would normally have found accommodation. Sons and daughters of existing tenants in particular are now finding that whereas in the past if there was a vacancy in the block they had been brought up in, through the Second Generation Scheme and others, they would have a chance of a flat, now, under the current policy, it is most likely to be boarded up until someone can afford to buy it. People with disabilities, who in the past would have been able to move off the thirteenth floor of a tower block, are now reduced to staying there or moving out of desperation and becoming a homeless persons' statistic. There is a whole new generation of people who are being made homeless who don't fit into the kind of stereotypes that people have of who homeless families are. On the Labour Group we spent a lot of time talking to existing tenants and explaining to them that the homeless people of today are the people who yesterday would have been their neighbours, to try and break down the stigmas that exist between tenants and homeless families.

There is this great Tory myth which is even now being shown to be a myth, that homelessness would be solved by breaking down the Rent Act; there is new housing legislation which is designed to allow private landlords to offer rents at market levels. The reality is that however high those market levels went, and even assuming you could find people who could afford to pay them, it is still not worthwhile to rent your property. These Tories need to be asked, 'If you had a house now empty, would you rent it or would you sell it?' Anyone with any financial sense at all would sell that property to an owner-occupier because of the tax incentives in owner-occupation, and because of the values of properties, particularly in London. So there is no evidence that offering rents at market levels will actually generate a private rented sector.

I know in countries like Sweden where you do have about 40 per cent of people living in rented accommodation it is made worthwhile to rent, not in terms of being able to chuck the tenant out when you feel like selling, but in terms of other tax advantages to the lessor. Here they very much want to leave housing to the private market and accept the wonders of market forces, but of course we know there is no evidence that freeing properties in the private rented sector is going to offer anything to those people who are homeless, because they do not have the financial resources to match the new rents, and also they will be very insecure as tenants. Now there is this new scheme, I think they call it

'The Business Enterprise Scheme'. The government will be using it to encourage more homes on to the private rented market, and to use that as a mechanism for encouraging tenants. Again I don't feel that that is going to meet the real demand, which is for fair-rented public sector subsidised housing, for which there is a huge demand, not just in London, but in rural areas in particular where people are really suffering. People whose children are born and raised in the rural areas are having to move, and have got no place at all for a future life within the communities they were raised in. The knock-on effect from London is spreading out into the rural areas where house prices are just extraordinary. I believe those things can only be tackled by local authorities operating through government funding and other means to provide affordable housing for people.

MM: How about what Patricia Kirwan says about repealing the Homeless Persons' Act and the Immigration Act?

JR: The key argument used by both Westminster Conservatives and by senior officers on their behalf, is that the best way to solve the homelessness problem is to repeal the Homeless Persons' Act. All that would do, if it came about, would be to change the requirements of who is counted as homeless. These people, however, will not disappear and my feeling is that whether someone is officially recognised as homeless or not doesn't make any difference to the fact that they have nowhere to live. Those people will still exist. Perhaps the effect will be that the figure will appear lower, in much the same way as the unemployment figures have been manipulated over the years. It will not stop us seeing people begging in the streets, or people living in cardboard boxes, so it is not a solution.

As far as immigration goes, since the new laws requiring people to apply for visas and everything else prior to entering the country, and having to go through all that bureaucracy at the point of exit from a nation, it seems amazing that anyone is able to get into Britain at all now, especially if they are black. It will always be possible to point at areas like Tower Hamlets, which historically have always been areas of high immigration, right through from the Irish community, and the Jewish community, and now to a new community, the Bangladeshi community. But that area of London is historically an impoverished area to which new immigrants have come; there will always be areas like that where you can point to high proportions of people from a minority ethnic community.

What we are trying to emphasise now is that there is a lot of homelessness amongst groups that people wouldn't normally identify as 'the homeless'; these are people whom we all know and who, not so many years ago, would have been housed. It is actually to avoid the problem to raise the immigration issue. There are many different types of people who are homeless, and it is wrong to concentrate on the immigration issue because it divides people along those lines when it is unnecessary. Tower Hamlets' problems are both historical and particularly financial; they are one of the poorest authorities who happen to be in an area which has traditionally been the first port of call for new immigrant communities. It is a shame that we haven't been able to recognise, with all the historical experience we have had up to now, that immigrant communities need the support of each other, particularly in a country like Britain which is perceived as racist, and that therefore they will choose to live near each other.

MM: Theresa Gorman asserted to me that it is really a question of gerrymandering and that Labour councils, when they built estates after the war, thought about where they needed more Labour votes, and she says, I think mistakenly, that by and large homeless people are Labour voters. I personally do not believe that they do vote, but that this has been taken into consideration in where they are rehoused.

JR: In Westminster we believe very strongly that the Designated Sales policy has grown specifically out of the fact that we came within 106 votes of winning the Council in 1986. There are 32 Tories on the Council and 27 of us and one Independent, so it is a Tory majority of four – five with the Lord Mayor's vote. The Council started off by believing that the 'Right to Buy' policies in themselves would create new Conservative voters. What they have now perceived is that in Westminster there are key areas where the large concentration in the form of a council estate has led to a natural support for Labour – which is not to say by any means that we can count on every council tenant vote, nor would we ever dream of saying we could. However, there is no doubt that if you start selling off council properties to people with the means, and if included in your list of who you would sell those properties to are people with the offer of a job in London, then you are paving the way for City gents to have a place that they own on a reasonably nice council estate, where they will stay in the week before they retreat to the country at the weekend, and we know by and large what those people vote. Now although in public session, in many cases, the majority group will deny that this is their view, it is quite clear from written documents like their 'Building Stable Community' statements, and from press interviews, that they think that people they believe have no economic role to play within the City of Westminster shouldn't live within the City of Westminster. Councillor Weeks is on video as saying that the two groups of people who need to live in Westminster are M Ps and waiters, and he also says on the same tape that people who do not have a job, or do not have anything to do in London could probably better live somewhere else. Now, although it would be wrong to ever assume as a Labour politician, that if you are unemployed, if you are homeless, or if you are low-waged, you are a natural Labour voter, or if you are a tenant you are a Labour voter, nevertheless, proportionally you can say the odds are more likely to be that people will vote a certain way. And this is no doubt what they are counting on.

We knew the policy would be a disaster, and it continues to be a disaster with over 500 homes empty that could be used today to house homeless people. They claim to have this huge list of people who said they were interested in buying. I don't deny that they probably do have a huge list of people. We know that where people have written down their income level, and that level is deemed to be not high enough to qualify, that those people remain on the list and are not told that their income is not high enough. So there is bound to be quite a proportion of those people on that list, who actually do not stand any chance of getting any of these properties. But the Council has proved incredibly incompetent and inefficient in doing this. Their Home Ownership policy actually now costs £7m. a year when you take into account the cost of the steel doors to board up.

The cost of the sales programme alone has put back the entire Council's programme in terms of the money it can spend on other things, like council properties. There has been an enormous overspend on the cost of the sales programme this year, and the extra cost projected for next year. If we look at the cost of staff salaries and the promotion and selling expenses that are related to the sale of council dwellings, there was an expenditure of £305,000 in 1986–7, that rose to £1,463,000 in 1987–8. The estimate for 1988–9 was originally £2,434,000 and the revised estimate for 1988–9 is £3,976,000. Now the reason for the difference between the estimates is mainly these metal doors that they put on the flats to keep out both squatters and tenants and the homeless. These doors cost £882,000 a year, just for the designated flats[1] – that is not for any flat that is going to be re-let, that is just for the designated flats. The loss of rent and rates on those properties alone is £863,000 for this year, but the real figure we expect will be a lot higher.

Those figures take no account either of the extra cost of the sales policy caused by the loss of the government housing subsidy that you get when you take these properties out of the rented sector, or the extra cost of the homeless accommodation provided for the increased number of homeless families. In the original Housing Committee

Report on this sales programme, the Treasurer said that those costs would come to about £3,122,000 in 1988–9, after the extra income from interests on the proceeds of the sales had been taken into account. That means that the *total* cost of the Designated Sales policy in 1988–9 is £7,000,000. Consequently the Council has just put up its rents to the tenants by 25 per cent, which will raise £6,775,000, and I don't think it is stretching a point too far to say that the rent increases being levied fund the cost of the sales programme.

So we have this huge figure for the extra cost for homeless families. When we raised these issues at the time of Designated Sales, the officers were quite clear that there would be an increase in homelessness, that it would be necessary therefore to find the money to provide alternative forms of accommodation for those homeless people. The politicians on the majority side made it clear that housing was a matter of priorities and that all local authorities decided where their priorities lay. Their priorities lay in meeting the huge demand for home ownership rather than the huge demand for housing *per se* or for a roof over one's head, and that basically is where the big ideological difference lies. I just very firmly believe that people have a right to a home regardless of any voting benefit that we might gain as a result of providing those homes. Those of us who put housing high on our agenda actually believe that in many ways housing and the lack of a home is even more of a contentious and difficult issue than unemployment. I certainly firmly believe that if you have no job, but you have a home to go back to after a day at the job centre or walking the streets, you can handle it. But if you have a job but you have nowhere to go at the end of the day, and you are living on your friends or your parents, or you are sharing with five other people in cramped conditions, that is very hard to survive emotionally. I think that in terms of the mental health of our nation we need to help these people by providing accommodation.

The use of bed and breakfast is clearly an absurd solution that has grown out of absurd circumstances. No one could ever say that it made economic sense to spend vast sums of money topping up the profits of hoteliers and bed and breakfast – breakfasteers – or whatever you call them. It is clearly ludicrous, but then none of the local authorities who are most renowned for spending the money on bed and breakfast have ever said anything other than that. The problem has been housing finance – councils have been forbidden to spend resources they have had on the necessary improvements to existing accommodation. They have not been allowed to spend the total of their capital receipts where they have them, but they have been allowed to spend money on bed-and-breakfast hotels, so what can they do? Obviously some councils have adopted a far more liberal or – I just call it socially minded – approach than others; consequently those authorities like Camden or Brent are the ones who can be shown to have huge numbers of homelessness. They are tightening up, although they don't want to.

Westminster is known to have one of the harshest policies on whom they accept as homeless within the legislation, allowing very little room for interpretation. There is no creative accounting when it comes to Westminster's view of who is homeless and who isn't. But even there, Westminster cannot deny that there are a large number of people going through their books who need help. But Westminster's approach, by being firm and unsympathetic, does tend to put people off and it is also a very hard thing for us to monitor. One doesn't want to be too intrusive into people's lives, and hound them when they leave the Homeless Persons' Centre and ask them, 'What response did you get from officers and what was going on?' I think these people are under enough pressure without us laying it on. I think, though, it is generally recognised throughout London, and among all the professional bodies that deal with homelessness and who have conducted surveys, that Westminster does offer one of the harshest interpretations; consequently its homeless figures appear lower than some of those boroughs who are more generous in their interpretation.

MM: What have the Labour Group on the Council been doing to protest against the new Housing Bill and the situation of the homeless and the housing crisis in general?

JR: We have a very strong group on the Housing Committee and I was part of that until last year, but I have moved to Social Services more recently. The main focus in more recent times to the issue of housing generally in Westminster has been the Designated Sales policy. We believe very strongly that protests should be people-led and tenant-led and not councillor-led. The most unusual feature of campaigning in Westminster has been on this estate where I live, where tenants have been using the Housing Act in a peculiar upside-down way, hoping to become the landlord and save homes for fair rent, as a way of subverting the attempts of the Council to sell properties. That's unique, but we have had a lot of encouraging support from the Labour Group and meetings have been held on all Council estates concerning Designated Sales in particular, and the effect it will have. There are posters that have appeared on a lot of steel doors which say, 'This home is for sale; where are your children going to live?' We believe that that is a point which can command as much support from as wide a section of the community as possible.

The problem we face with regard to Westminster's homeless is that

129

they are not placed within Westminster any more – the Council by and large now moves them to hostels and areas like Dagenham, and I don't know where else. We led a very successful campaign against the proposal to build prefabricated houses in Bexley, with the support of the Council there and Brian Gould who is the local MP, on an area which had been designated for a power station. What we have concentrated on is the fact that unlike so many of the other inner London boroughs, Westminster has the resources to deal with its housing problem to a large extent, but chooses not to do so, chooses to place it elsewhere. So we work mainly closely with tenants' groups where we can. We have a mobile display that can be offered to any tenants' group who wishes to borrow it which explains the policy and what people can do to fight it, although it is an uphill struggle – it is not an easy task to beat a majority group on the Council.

MM: How do you think the new Housing Bill is going to affect the homeless?

JR: The area I am most up on in the Housing Bill is the key area supposedly called 'Tenants' Choice' – Section 4 of the Bill – where private landlords can buy up estates and take them off the councils' hands. The aim of the Housing Bill is to turn councils into 'enablers' rather than providers of supposedly affordable housing. I personally think that we needn't worry about the Housing Bill in terms of tenants' choice; I'm encouraged by the ballots that have been held amongst tenants up and down the country who have voted to remain with their council. Another part of me sees it as a positive thing that councillors have been forced to look to the level of provision and service they give and to say, 'Well, what are the good points about being a council tenant and what are the bad points and what can we do to improve on the bad points?', in order to encourage a 'yes' vote to stay with the council amongst our communities. So far the results have been very good, with notable gains of tenants, like in Torbay and also the Housing Action Trust (HAT) areas gaining the right to vote over whether they want a HAT set up or not. These are huge achievements from the tenants' movement from groups of people who are normally not identified as having those sort of strengths.

I don't see that the Housing Act will do anything to benefit the homeless; under Section Four we are going to be dealing with properties that are already tenanted by and large. If they are taken into the private sector it will only be worthwhile for a developer if parts of those properties, as they become empty, are for people with income who can purchase them, otherwise why would any developer possibly want to take on a council estate? So I just see the homeless being completely marginalised under the new Housing Act and that there will be very little change. Of course, the key change will be the consequence of 'Right to Buy' and all the other policies involved in selling off council estates – that the overall availability of stock that homeless people can go to is reduced daily. Councils will be left with the slummiest, the worst of all available housing. I suspect the Government accepts that will happen, and are happy for that to happen; it will be like the workhouse or the Poor Law, this last remnant of grotty housing which the Council will be responsible for, and where the destitute will be placed – the totally destitute will be left to roam the streets, I suspect.

MM: But councils will still have this obligation to house the homeless, won't they?

JR: I wouldn't be surprised to see some sort of repeal of the homelessness legislation, over the next year. It is not going to do anything except change the requirement to house people who need housing. The housing crisis is going to get progressively worse, and I think the consequence of that will be that there will need to be a change in tack, politically, as there was in the 1950s – you know it was no accident that Macmillan was the person who started to build houses. I think it is interesting to note that there is probably more interest in housing now. Clive Soley, the Labour housing spokesperson, has been able to get a considerable amount of coverage for the opposition view. The non-quality press hasn't as yet taken up all the issues, largely because it doesn't affect the people who write for those papers or the people who own those papers or run them. However, I think as more and more people who show the acceptable face of homelessness, in terms of those newspapers, appear with terrible stories of how it is affecting their lives and we can get in that human element with statistics and figures, we will be able to get coverage. When we are able to prove that this family here, whom everyone would love as a neighbour, has nowhere to live, specifically because of this policy, we may be able to see the tabloids taking up the issues. If mortgages continue to rise as well, which will clearly affect a much larger proportion of people than council tenants, then again that will raise the profile of housing.

I think the problem that we face at the moment in terms of public awareness of the issue is that housing problems are still all looked at separately. The problems of owner-occupiers and mortgages, leases and repairs and the difficulties they have with their private freeholders, the problems of council tenants, and the problems of the homeless – what they add up to is a crisis of housing in Britain today, and that has yet to strike the media. If things continue I think it is inevitable that the main broadcasting media and others will look on this as a key crisis; we are certainly working to try and encourage these different groups of people to see that they have a common interest in seeing a general review and repeal of all housing legislation with a view to solving the problem. It is hard to bring those groups of people together. Divide and rule is an old Tory ploy, and it works very well in housing as in everything else. But the issue definitely has a much higher profile than it did certainly in 1986 when I was elected, and in the Labour Party in particular the issue is considered far more important. We are beginning to feel heartened that more and more people are beginning to take it seriously and in part the Housing Act has done that.

MM: Now if in 1990 the Conservative very small majority is turned into a Labour one, what do you think will change on Westminster Council, apropos of housing?

JR: The key things that will change are the priorities that we set ourselves. Local government is so constrained now by central government dictat that, without breaking the law or without completely fiddling the books, we will need to look very carefully at what we can do. I can imagine within the first week of the Labour administration in Westminster, the steel doors will be removed from 500 (or by then perhaps 750–1000) boarded properties and the equivalent number of people who fit the needs for those homes on the Council's housing list will be housed. We will certainly use all the planning controls that we can to free all the properties that are kept empty on the private sector, for use by council tenants. Now that's a problem – it is a problem for councils, because we know there are many more homes in the private sector empty than in the public sector. Planning restrictions, however, make it quite difficult at the moment to just go in and compulsorily purchase empty properties. I think we would have to use some of these lease-back arrangements that some councils have made with the private sector, where you pay them a certain sum to use their properties for a while, and hand them back at some stage later. We would need to bide our time, making as much provision as possible for our homeless people and our overcrowded people, which in Westminster is a big, big problem, until hopefully the next Labour government can ease our situation first by freeing us from the capital restraints that we all have, allowing us to spend more money in the areas that we want to and second by repealing the Housing Acts which actually frustrate a council's ability to do anything. But certainly the Designated Sales policy would go.

We have never really seen the Right to Buy as a threat in Westminster. We believe that the vast majority of the people who can afford to buy have now done so. In Westminster that is a very low figure, because property values limit how much discount you can get – it actually does limit the number of people that can buy. The Housing Act has sadly had the effect of encouraging people who really don't have the means to buy to go into ownership. Many have no conception what it means to be faced with a service charge and a repairs bill, when in the past they just rang up the Council who came to repair any damage. I feel very strongly that we should remind council tenants about this, because however appalling your local council is about getting the repairs done, in the end they do get it done and that is what you pay your rent for. If you buy a property, you are liable for all those repairs. On a lot of the larger estates where people are buying, if the Council has plans to do a major refurbishment programme, although the Council know about it in advance, now by law tenants who buy subsequently are still liable for their share of costs of that refurbishment, although the rest of the tenants have already paid for it through their rent. I think there are a lot of disadvantages in being a home-owner on a council estate, particularly in Westminster where the designated 'right-to-buy' prices are often coming in cheaper than market value: if you already own and you want to sell you may find that the steel-doored flat identical to yours next door is being offered a lot cheaper, frustrating your attempts to sell. If and when we win the Council next year we will want to look at ways of helping all sectors in housing.

MM: What would you do to help people in bed and breakfast?

JR: What we can do is put a much higher priority on the environmental health aspects of the role of Social Services and Education, and lead the way in co-ordinating approaches across boroughs. I know that the London Boroughs Association and Association of London Authorities have working parties that have been working for years and years on trying to get agreements between all boroughs on the approach to bed-and-breakfast. So that, for instance, if Haringey Council decides that Hotel A is completely unfit for human habitation, that the next day Ealing Council will not house someone there. Unfortunately, in a lot of cases, for every step forward that has been taken in that, Westminster has taken a step backward, trying to subvert that sort of agreement, which I know is frustrating for officers.

One of the great tragedies of the demise of the G L C is the role it could have played as a strategic authority, looking at problems associated with homelessness across the whole of London and being able to circumvent individual councils' personal preferences for the greater good of the homeless. Closing down the hostels and bed-and-breakfast hotels is not going to solve anything because while councils are not allowed to spend their money in any other way we are still left

133

with the problem of what to do with the homeless. But as the Local Authority responsible for environmental health we could beef up our Environmental Health Department so that it really had teeth. Westminster at the moment has a very good environmental health system in my opinion, the officers work very hard; it is just not big enough, nor are there enough workers for the work that needs to be done.

MM: You could close down the hotels that were infested with cockroaches, for instance.

JR: Right, and if not closing them down, getting rid of the infestations, straight away.

MM: Don't you think that that should be the responsibility of Westminster City Council, not just of the councils that are using the hotel?

JR: I think it should; but whose statutory responsibility it is is not straightforward.

An area I am particularly interested in at the moment is the consequences of the new education proposals on homeless families. If you are a child of Ealing and you are living in Westminster, do you have to be bused to Ealing every day for your education when Ealing becomes an education authority in its own right, as does Westminster? In areas where there are people from one authority living under the roof of another, it needs to be very clear whose responsibility those children are, and in these cases it should always be the interest of the child, not the interest of the local authority, that should come first.

There has been criticism of the I L E A that they haven't been able to deal with the problem of children living in hotels. There is a vast number of children that no one knows about, that are not being educated. Again I would like to think that when Labour run the Department of Education in 1990, we will say, 'Let's find out how many children there are; can we place these children in our schools, if there is nowhere else, and if not at least *identify* them, and then pass this information on?' I accept that it would be wrong to expect Westminster to be responsible for all those families, but it could certainly pass on the information they can get so much more easily than the other authorities. It needs a lead co-ordinator – the G L C would have been ideally placed to offer that role. There are working groups that cut across political lines, but the politics get in the way.

MM: Do you think people ought to be able to choose where they want to live?

JR: Within reason, yes. It seems obvious to me that the key to a successful housing policy should be choice. Choice is a Conservative catchphrase, but they choose to apply it only if you can afford it. We believe people should have choice as a right, where practicable. If the whole world decided they all wanted to live in Oxford Street we would have a problem, but that isn't how it works – people have different preferences and by and large they should be met. In the private sector, where people can afford to buy limits their choice of a home. But that is very different from saying to a family whose entire community network and support is in one area, 'You have got to move a hundred miles or to the other side of the country, or to a borough you know nothing about, or you have to move on to an all-white estate and risk racial harassment and petrol bombs being thrown through your letterbox.' I think it is quite acceptable for people to state their preferences. I think it is equally acceptable, however, to have a range of preferences so it at least gives officers and workers some scope. People need to be flexible. I don't want to go casting aspersions, but I don't believe these councillors act with the best interests of the people in Hounslow; I think it is more who they would like as neighbours and who they would not, and that is wrong.

MM: Can you give me some examples of the ways in which Westminster have mismanaged housing and the homeless?

JR: There are some very good examples of how their priority in terms of selling off stock completely contradicts all semblance of morality when it comes to what housing should be available. We have an estate called the Townshend Estate, which was designated for sale. That means that as a flat becomes vacant, it is boarded up until someone can buy it, rather than it being available for offer. A large number of flats on the Townshend Estate were specially adapted for the use of people with disabilities, with handrails in place, extra-wide doors and bathrails already there. There was a petition from the residents of the Townshend Estate, many of whom were home-owners, saying that it was completely outrageous that these places should be sold because they were specifically designed for a group of people who never got housing adequate to their needs. They also felt at the time that it was illegal to do this, although the Council's advice was otherwise. When the Council puts a steel door on property, it usually also smashes up the property internally in order to prevent squatters from using any of the amenities, if they did get in. In Townshend they ripped out all the specially-adapted features, in this instance obviously not to prevent squatters getting in but to make the building more attractive to the able-bodied community who were purchasing.

This estate where I live is a series of Victorian terraced houses, plus two tower blocks. There has been a campaign going on for four years to prevent it being sold either lock, stock and barrel to a private developer, or as part of a barter deal where half of the estate would be sold off in return for the other half being repaired. The main emphasis of the campaign has been holding the community together; the fact is that the community didn't want to be altered to the point at which every other door had a 'For Sale' notice on it and was part of the yuppy market. We very much wanted to remain together as a community in public-sector housing.

MM Have any of the houses been sold round here?

JR: No. In a period of four years we have managed to avoid that; other than 'Right to Buys' which are people's individual right, not one home has been sold. One of the tower blocks on this estate, Chancery Point, at present has eight residents left in it. The rest of the block – it houses 101 flats – has been systematically destroyed by the Council to prevent squatting or any other form of occupation. Toilets have been ripped out, bathrooms have been ripped out; the block is known to be riddled with asbestos so there is a twofold danger, not only to the structural integrity of the building, but that asbestos is actually being released into the air. What is more poignant is that if the eight residents who still live there can *stay* there, and put up with the destruction all around them and the deliberate attempt to encourage them to move out, those eight residents will be able to secure that block for the rest of the tenants on Walterton, when we apply to take over the estate. Under the Housing Act legislation, in a block, as opposed to a house, as long as there is one single qualifying tenant that whole property counts. So the Council is frantic to move those people out prior to the date at which we apply to take over the estate. We will know if we are an approved landlord by 20 March, and very soon after that we will put in our bid, and the bid date is the date by which everything else is judged. So were the Council successful in moving everyone out only *after* that date, it wouldn't matter, that block would still be ours. Eight people on the front line, defending housing for rent which is being systematically destroyed around them; every flat has partition walls being smashed down. Generally on this estate and in the Victorian houses all toilets and bathrooms are removed. What is so ironic and horrendous about this is that there are still tenants on this estate who do not have access to their own bathrooms, or access to their own toilet. They share with other people and they know that next door to them is a house that had a bathroom which is being ripped out.

Those are two examples of the Council's approach to housing generally. As far as homelessness is concerned, the Council has been trying to use its powers through the Planning Committee to close down bed-and-breakfast hotels, or try and insist that they can't be used for homeless families. It is a dilemma; on the one hand it's good, because we don't like the bed-and-breakfast places, but on the other hand it doesn't solve the problem that the Council is facing with homelessness. What they have done at the same time is to write letters to the actual homeless persons in those bed-and-breakfast hotels informing them what they are doing, which obviously is very intimidatory for people. So you are living in this appalling place and then you get a letter from Westminster City Council saying, 'We just thought you ought to know that we are taking the landlord to court with a view to closing down his premises!' It makes insecurity out of insecurity, and must be absolutely awful.

I think they are hoping people will move out. They would like to see homeless families putting pressure on their own authorities – 'Get me out of this hotel; it is about to be closed.' What also happens is that some people just give up and can't take it any more, and they find themselves alternative accommodation, which might mean sleeping with ten other people on a neighbour's floor. They give up attempting to get into secure accommodation.

MM: So the Council are trying to empty the bed-and-breakfast hotels.

JR: There is no doubt that is what they want to do. The members who represent key areas like Bayswater and Lancaster Gate went on a major offensive in all their election publicity against the noisy, disruptive, smelly and generally horrendous behaviour they said was coming from homeless families. They used them as a target to gain political support, and generally victimised them in a subtle Tory way. I am not accusing them of going round to anyone with a sledgehammer personally, but this is the approach they have. What Westminster actually does with its own homeless is export them, and it becomes more and more difficult to raise the issue of the homeless in Westminster. By the time you raise the issue those families are over in Dagenham. They would certainly argue that it is because of cost, but we know that the previous Chair of Housing – there have been about five in the last four years – Councillor Hartley, was quite clear in his mind that he wanted no homeless families in Westminster, and the finances were not really relevant to that. We know from documents we have seen, that we shouldn't have as it were. What he was interested in was getting rid of these people from the environs of Westminster.

Under the Housing Act, we see that the legislation was designed to encourage private landlords to take estates off Labour councils, in particular. In order to offer incentives to the private landlord to take on the estates, given the bad condition many estates are in, an interesting device was arranged within the Act to do with the valuation of the estate at the point of transfer, and the interesting thing about the valuation is that it isn't the value of the properties *per se*, but the value of the properties less all their repair needs. That can actually mean that the properties are in such bad condition that an estate has a *negative* value and our rough figures at the moment for this estate, including the tower blocks, estimate that the Council would need to give us a dowry, as it is called in the Act, of £30,000,000. Obviously the next question to ask is, 'Where are the Council to get this money from?' Our answer at the moment is, 'Well, that is really for the Council and the Secretary of State to work out. It is amusing because it's between us and Westminster Council, and we will be able to preserve our community if it comes off. It will not be amusing if it is applied to Labour authorities.

If the tenants become the freeholder of the estate we will then hand over housing management to a local housing association. We won't become a co-operative, because we don't have any intention of managing the estate ourselves – there is far too much work that needs doing, it would be much too much for the tenants themselves. We would employ a housing association to do that. We have made it quite clear that we will operate a full equal-opportunity policy, that we will have to have assured tenancies, that we will have our own tenancy agreement which will be a Fair Rent Tenancy Agreement along the lines of most housing association tenants. Finally, when homes are repaired and are vacant, we will house people from the Council along these lines.

On 24 April 1989, Jackie Rosenberg told me that on 20 March, after a three-year campaign, they successfully served notice to acquire their estate under the new Housing Act. Westminster City Council are contesting their negative valuation of £30m. and claiming the dowry should only be £15m.

PART THREE

Interviews with women who work with homeless families

These four women all work closely with homeless people. June Bowie is the head of a Paddington primary school where many of the homeless families send their children. Shelagh O'Brien helps to run the Drop-In Centre which is the only social outlet for many of the women stranded with children in bed-and-breakfast hotels. Both are well-known local figures who work with great dedication at difficult jobs.

Angela Taft's research for the World Health Organisation did not bring her into such close daily contact with homeless people, but her analytical approach to the health problems of women in bed-and-breakfast is valuable. Like Jackie Rosenberg, she concludes that gerrymandering is at the heart of Westminster's housing policies. Mary Tester runs the Westminster Homeless Persons' Unit. She is a bureaucrat, understandably cautious about uttering any criticism of the Government which employs her.

June Bowie

June Bowie is the Head of St James and St Michael Infants and Junior School, a Church of England school in Paddington. In 1988 105 out of the 160 children in the school were living in bed-and-breakfast hotels. Local teachers like June are only too aware of the conditions these children live in. Interviewed in the *Independent*, Dr Sue Jenkins, the paediatrician at Hallfield, another local school, said, 'In the first hotel for the homeless I ever went into, I was able to count five health hazards within the first few minutes. There were broken banisters, broken windows, and live wires hanging from the ceiling. Rat poison was lying on the kitchen floor in open saucers . . . Living in these conditions can sometimes cause serious behavioural problems. Although it is wrong to generalise, the younger children cooped up in hotel rooms eight hours a day become very depressed. They regress. We see a lot of children with speech and language problems because they are very understimulated. They tend to act up, to become wild and aggressive and difficult to control.'

In the same article Michael Morland, Head at North Westminster School, a secondary school with 120 hotel children, described their learning difficulties as 'the most appalling social and educational problem I have known since studying education since the war'.[1]

Many school-age children living in the hotels don't go to school, either because they are turned away from overcrowded ones or because their parents think they will only be in the hotels for a brief period. Other parents don't speak enough English to be able to cope with finding a school.

June Bowie estimated that each class in her school admits two children and loses two each week. When I interviewed her in 1988, 75 per cent of the children at the school were Bangladeshi. The toy library where I worked was originally housed in the basement of June Bowie's school, so I met her several times before I interviewed her. She is 58, divorced, with grown-up children, and lives with her mother.

The interview took place in June's office, upstairs in the school, which is decorated with the children's work. She is, for a head teacher, unusually accessible to both children and staff, who all call her by her first name. The day I interviewed her she was nervous, partly because she dislikes being interviewed and also because she was under great stress; her son had just had a car accident and she was also desperately anxious about the results of the parental ballot, organised by parents angry that they had had no say in the Government's decision to abolish I L E A, which was about to take place.

I've been Head of this school since January 1980, when of course it was quite a different school in many ways. It always had a certain mobility, and I suppose it must have been in the early 1980s that we noticed that the mobility was increasing. We then learned that families were being put into bed-and-breakfast accommodation, and I can remember, very early on, having a meeting at this school about homelessness. People from all the boroughs who were sending families into the hotels in Westminster were at the meeting. So, very early on, there was an awareness that this was happening, and of course it has just increased. At its height there would be anything from five to six hundred children of primary-school age whose names and addresses we knew, who would at any one time be waiting for a vacancy in the school. Sometimes of course they waited for as long as a year. That situation continued until September 1987, when we suddenly noticed there was a change. People started being rehoused, not as they had originally intended in flats that had been suitably decorated or whatever but being sent back to flats that hitherto would not have been acceptable, just to get rid of the homelessness problem.

There are some obvious special problems the children living in the hotels have. If you live in one room, sometimes as many as six children and parents, then there are going to be areas of difficulty. They don't have cooking facilities; very little chance to play in the normal way, to help Mother or Father do the normal things; or indeed for older children to be able to do their homework.

However, all children come to school with various degrees of problems and one has to be very careful not to categorise the children. All one can do is give them the possibilities that they lack at home: the possibilities for play, to redress the balance. I think it's very important that we don't think of children in different categories. We welcome all children, from whatever culture they come, from whatever faith, from whatever social stratum, and it's our aim to meet the needs of these children. In the first instance, the educational needs, but of course this is so much tied up with social needs too. And to this end we have taken certain steps; that is to say, we have always been convinced that it's essential to have a welcoming ethos, so that children will learn to play together, work together, live together, be sensitive to each other's needs, be sensitive to each other's faith and cultures, and to learn about each other. This is the most important thing, I think, from the point of view of an equitable society. So, great emphasis is put on that, and to this end we have tried to break down barriers.

We try to help all the children to feel at home, so that there is something of their culture that they will see here and recognise and feel familiar with, whether it is people or pictures or books or texts, or whatever. And also that they know they will be valued as individuals.

About six years ago, we decided that we would dispense with titles. If we don't give the children a title, why should they give us a title? Besides which, for those of us who are Christians, it is indeed calling each other by our names in Christ, because in fact, when you think about it, those are the only names that we have. The others belong to our fathers. People did say, 'Mmm, what about discipline?' I don't like using the word discipline, because I feel that you can't command respect or anything else; you have to earn it. I think this is another very important philosophy that we have here. How can it make any difference what you call somebody? I know there's an authoritarian tradition, but we aim to help the children to become independent.

We have felt concerned for a long time about what happens at playtimes, and about what playtimes are for. Of course there is a certain amount of aggression at playtimes. We have always given the children the possibility of having a quiet playtime, because we feel that this is very important for them; children who feel threatened, who feel that it's a fraught situation out there. So although we have two playgrounds, which means the staff have always accepted that they do double duty, they elected to have three duties every day to give the children this facility. But we were still concerned. Quite often we found that the children wouldn't want to go out to play at all, because they were involved in what they were doing. And, of course, coming back from play, people felt that a lot of time was wasted because then they had to be settled down all over again, because they were high coming in from playtime and so on. I think we were the third school to run an integrated day.

Families are moved on, sometimes at 24 hours' notice. Children just disappear – we aren't always notified. It is upsetting. But it's amazing what you get used to. It's amazing what children get used to, and they adjust. As I say, there's always been a mobility rate, and when I first came here I questioned the Head that I was taking over from. I actually said, 'It must be very frustrating.' And she said, 'Well, no. You can't look at it like that. We just accept that we're here and you have to do what you can.' And I think this is really what's happened; we feel that, as a Church school, we're here to meet the needs of the community.

Although I suppose 75 per cent of our children, or more, are not Christian, the Christian element has increased of late. Partly due to the Irish coming over. Very many more children are coming from Ireland via Camden, being sent into Westminster, to the hotels. On the other hand until recently the preponderance of our bed-and-breakfast families have been from Bangladesh, where they have a very stable family background. They come without the kind of social problems that other children might bring from what might be considered to be a more normal background, from, you know, a flat or a house. I welcome the fact that we have a lot of Moslems in the school, because I think it's a very important learning situation for all of us.

The use of bed-and-breakfast accommodation, I have said very loud and very often and in quite public places, although it's never been reported, I feel is a scandal which will mar this age historically. It is utterly sickening, when you think of the money that is spent on it, and lining people's pockets, when that money could be used.

But what I also want to say is, that we are very committed to what we're doing in education. It extends beyond one's wildest dreams of what one would have thought one's job was. It's so open-ended that there are no parameters: you just feel that you have to go on and on. I leave home at seven-thirty, and very often I'm not home until seven, sometimes seven-thirty; I would say ninety per cent of the time I am certainly not home before six-thirty. I go home weighed under with work. It is by far the biggest part of my life.

My children are grown up, my baby will be thirty in April! I have my 92-year-old mother living with me. She came to live with me six years ago. I feel very sorry for her, because she has moved from a little Welsh village, and she doesn't see anybody. Then when I go home, either I fall asleep on her bed or I have a meal with her and then I go; but at least it's better than her being totally on her own.

I shall be sixty next year. I'm not saying that I shall retire, because at the moment I can't think of it. It just seems too impossible to leave all this. But on the other hand I also have to think of my health. So I'm not actually making any decision just yet.

I have on many occasions gone to a rally or whatever else, or to conferences to speak or, in my case, read a paper, something that is a total anathema to me, but I feel nevertheless I have to do it. Although

I'm leaving school to do so and I feel that this should not be happening, I have said, on the two occasions I've been to a conference, that if all the efforts of the people at that day conference were channelled into protesting straight back to central government about housing policies, I do honestly feel that the energies would be used in a better way than us propping up an iniquitous system which is what we're doing, in a sense. What I am fighting for is for people to have a right to a home, for people to have the right to free education, for people to have the right to a health service, for people to have the right to work – all of these areas have been and are being deliberately eroded by this present Government.

In meeting the needs of these children, I L E A are very generous. I could not have asked for more. I mean – I didn't want to say that – I always ask for more! But they have supported me in every possible way, and of course now that the Government is cutting their budget, forcing them to cut their budget, I don't know what's going to happen. I know what is happening at the moment: they are trying to bury the evidence in whatever way they can, and sending people back to homes that are totally inadequate. Here in Bayswater and Paddington certain things have happened; there has been funding to support the Bayswater Homelessness Project. This is a pressure group which has done a lot of good work, although it's gone largely unrecognised by the people we would hope to impress by it.

The homeless are disenfranchised. They cannot be insured, so I've known of cases where people's total worldly belongings have gone up in smoke and they can't get a penny for it. I'm very concerned at the moment with the parental ballot that is taking place when every parent is going to have the possibility of making a gesture. I really fear that a lot of my parents won't get this opportunity, because they're moved from hotel to hotel, and the addresses I give aren't necessarily the ones that they are in at this present moment. I questioned this – I rang up the parents' group that are organising it, and said, 'Could you let me have some ballot papers so that I can give them to people who haven't received them?' Of course that isn't possible, because obviously anyone could then say they haven't had one, and then they could have two.

I L E A has been in the forefront of trying to provide for an equitable society with their initiatives on equal opportunities and anti-racism. One has read just this week that Kensington and Chelsea are actually intending to drop those sort of initiatives. The thing that concerns me most about it all is that it's going to be so divisive. And also that I can't understand that people are going to accept that there are going to be enormous cuts in education. If they're not going to put their money into education, it makes me very, very depressed.

My job has become more and more demanding. We opened a community room because we want to feel that the school is part of the community, and we want the community to feel that they are part of the school; so we have adult-education classes: sewing, English as a second language. In the past we've had all sorts of things. We've had six-week workshops for parents on maths in school, or whatever. We've had movement classes for staff, pupils and parents after school. We've had a family group, run by parents. We involved community groups and we got some parents to do a course and become able to run their own family groups. I suppose I see our role as rather like what the Church used to be. Well, I wouldn't want to compare it to a Church, because it's élitist, in a sense. I wouldn't want us to be élitist. We are open to whoever wants to use us.

In February 1989 I spoke to June again. She had decided to retire very soon, at 60, and said that her job had become much harder in the intervening year. The Inner London Education Authority, whose policies she had fervently supported, was about to disappear. ILEA had set up a Homeless Families Team but no more referrals could be made to it because of a three-month backlog of work. Social workers were leaving 'in droves' and teachers were demoralised by the threat of the unknown as the running of schools will pass to the local boroughs.

Note

1 *Independent*, 23 September 1987.

Angela Taft

Angela is an Australian who has lived in London for 16 years. Her children have grown up here but she reluctantly plans to return to Australia because she feels so pessimistic about the situation in England. She is a warm woman of 38, with grey hair and a strong face.

Angela is working on a report for the World Health Organisation, a study of links between homelessness and health. We talked in her office, in an annexe of St Mary's Hospital, Paddington.

In our report we're looking at the development of the Bayswater Project and how it has been a response to the situation in the area. We're one of the most hard-hit areas in the entire country, because so many of the London boroughs are sending their homeless families into this area; we have such a dense population of bed-and-breakfast hotels. The report is looking at the way in which the project is assisting homeless families, the way it is monitoring legislation and the councils' responses to it, and the way it is monitoring the Health Authority's response. We are looking at how it's helping families actually to articulate their own feelings about homelessness and to be involved in the campaign and to take control of their lives, and to try and make an impact on policy at every level. My specific interest (from my other work, which is on the Health Authority) is how the H A is itself responding to the problem of homelessness. We're very aware of the cost in management and financial and human terms of the service in this area. It's changed the face of it quite dramatically.

The Government said to us in the Stoker Report: 'You should be getting rid of some of your excess accommodation' – which, of course, in London in the 1980s is a joke. Accommodation is so expensive that low-paid staff can't afford to buy. So we don't really have any excess, but because of the financial pressure, and because of the shortage of people we need desperately like nurses and medical secretaries, the H A itself is now looking at its own accommodation. Many years ago – 20 years ago in some cases – when we brought out foreign workers to work as domestics, we offered them tied accommodation. Now the H A is in the position of saying to these women, 'Terribly sorry, but we need this accommodation and you'll have to leave it.' So we are in the ludicrous and contradictory position of threatening our own staff with homelessness in an area where this is a critical health problem. The staff are devastated! The women that my fellow Authority members and I have been visiting are women who were brought out here many years ago from areas of Spain – mainly Spain and Portugal. They have given years of their working life. They're single women, they're low-paid, and this has been their life, this is their community. They've been living in that accommodation for many, many years, so they are devastated. And rather lost, and very sad, and, with the stronger members, really quite angry. Quite rightly.

There's very little they can do, they are powerless on the whole, as most low-paid workers are. The situation here is that Westminster City Council have frozen their lists, so there's no chance for them. They will be put on the Council waiting list. Many of them are in the terrible situation of having lost their jobs, because the Health Service was instructed to privatise as much as possible. Of course, the easiest and quickest to privatise are domestic workers because they are low-paid and poorly organised. Our catering and cleaning jobs were put out to tender and the private contractors who came back basically took people on saying that they were paying the same amount. But they were asking staff to work longer hours, and also staff lost their rights to pensions and lost all their other bargaining rights over their wages. Some of these women said, 'Look, I can't work like that,' and went on to Social Security. They don't have jobs, so therefore it's even more difficult to find alternative accommodation.

London accommodation is outrageous. You just can't get a single room for under £40, £50, up to £100 a week. So that's out. Kensington and Chelsea have a waiting list, of at least 10,000 I think – so council accommodation, really, is pretty well out. We wouldn't have a problem of homelessness if all other accommodation – housing associations – weren't full to the gills. They are basically very, very frightened women, because they don't know what's going to happen to them. The Health Authority's Personnel Department hate what they're doing. They haven't issued notices to quit, because that would put them on a legal footing of actually evicting. They don't want to evict.

Westminster's housing policy is that, in line with Government policy and instructions, they are selling off 50 per cent of their housing stock, which of course is going to reduce the public housing. I know that they have 1,000 Category A, that is highest medical need people, who are waiting to be either housed or rehoused.

If one was politically cynical, one would say, 'Well, they are enabling wealthy people who would support Tory policies to buy into the area, thus changing the political complexion.' Sort of gerrymandering by another door. They are basically saying, 'We're not interested in homelessness. These people are not the kind of people we want.' So they've got this wonderful idea of making a mobile shanty town; I call it a shanty town, because a shanty town basically doesn't have all the support services. They're trying to shift them as far out of Greater London as they can: they've tried Barking and Haringey. I don't think they're going to get housing permission. They're just trying to buy up wasteland sites. Wonderful. Extraordinary. There's a very nice piece of graffiti, actually, outside what used to be St Mary's Hospital in the Harrow Road, where there's this wonderful new marina and glamorous housing development project. Somebody's written, 'Homes for the yuppies and caravans for the homeless.' In a sort of bitter way that's the truth, really. Luckily we've made an agreement that they will build 420 nurses' homes on that site. So we are waiting, and I keep hoping that they'll do those quickly. It may make some impact on our own homeless, and maybe provide some answer for the domestic workers. That remains to be seen.

There was a sit-in last year, which was supported by London Health Emergency and other groups wanting to support these women. In fact, with the lobby on the H A itself of sympathetic members, we managed to overturn that decision. Unfortunately, nine months later, they brought it back; they slipped it in after a very gruelling Authority meeting – it was Item 10 on the agenda and it simply said 'Accommodation' and we were really not warned. It was overturned, and we were absolutely devastated by that. So we – the members of the Authority who feel very angered by this decision – will try and reverse it in the next few months. What happens depends on whether we are merged with Brent. That would mean an enormous new health authority, from the Harrow Road to well past the North Circular. It will have the same number of Health Authority members, and the Regional Health Authority's made it clear that they're going to vet, and they're already vetting: and troublemakers like us'll be off. So we may not have a say, frankly.

I got involved in health issues, and certainly I've always been involved with minorities, probably because my father was a refugee. I've always been interested in women's health issues and from that a friend of mine who was involved in Labour women's politics with me said, 'Please would you come on to the Health Authority.' I had a long, hard think because I knew it was a lot of hard work and finally I thought, Well, I'm really very interested and committed, so I will concentrate my energies on that area of political work.

I've been here 16 years. When I first came over I was teaching in secondary education and I was involved in family planning and general studies and women's issues. And that's shifted, really; my interest in women's health has grown. Women's health is tied up with their housing, is tied up with their employment, their income, their confidence.

My research work is involved in looking at community development – 'approaches to health promotion' – that's very jargonish. But health promotion is a new way of looking at health issues, broadening its perspective, to include the whole socio-economic background to health and to try and make the Health Service acknowledge that there are many things outside its remit which affect health, over which it has no controls. How is it going to make links? How is it going to respond? How do we need to alter health policy to take account of all that? How does the Health Service make the Government listen? How does it advocate to the Government its responsibilities about health? How does it make it recognise its housing policies, its economic policies, all the different policies which make an impact on health? Our own project is looking at this on a small, district level, and looking at community development, which is really how to involve the community, how to involve people in their own health. What does that mean for health policy? What does it mean for getting people to become involved?

I work on something called 'Health for All 2000', which is a World Health Organisation initiative. Now, in our district we have all the inner-city problems *in extremis*: we have a crisis of homelessness; we have a very high suicide rate, 200 per cent the national average; we have a very high level of drug abuse; we have a high number of single mothers; 40 per cent of our district are ethnic minorities, some of whose first language isn't English; we have, because of the expertise of this teaching hospital, an enormously high A I D S caseload; we have a crisis of housing. All inner-city problems.

The Health Service in our area is consistent with others in that it's underfunded. The Working Party has decided they ought to take money from Westminster and give it to outer counties. So it means we lose, all the time. We lose because of our staffing costs, which are basically about 70–80 per cent of our costs, because the Government doesn't fund it properly. The N H S inflation is at least 3 or 4 per cent above ordinary inflation, but the Government only fund us for the ordinary inflation. We also have enormous needs, say for A I D S funding, that we weren't, until the last few months, properly funded for. So the Health Service in this area is in crisis, we have enormous needs and we have Tory councillors selling off the public housing stock.

I think things are getting worse. I've been reading about housing legislation and future Government proposals and what the lobbies, who know a great deal more about it than I do, are saying. They are saying that the new Housing Bill that's going through Parliament is devastating. I was looking at the Bayswater Project's own response to the White Paper – which is very detailed, and I think very good – and they've pointed out that the deregulation of the private sector, added to the existing policy of selling off council homes, the way in which council tenants really won't be consulted properly, the power that's being given to landlords, is very, very depressing news. I think what you're going to see is a real increase in homelessness. Added to that, I don't see the Health Service's finances yet being put on any better footing. I wish I could say that I could see a political leader on the horizon – or a party – in a fit enough condition to tackle Mrs Thatcher. But I don't see that either. So I'm very gloomy about it, yes.

I've had contact with the Health Service employees who are dealing with the health problems of families in bed-and-breakfast. I know the more active women who've taken on a campaigning role and they are aware and articulate. It's all those thousands of women who don't get out that I feel very much more concerned about. I do, because of my work, read reports about the conditions for women. I know what the health workers have said and how health visitors feel, how difficult it is to communicate, how difficult it is to make contact, the lack of contact and communications from councils to let them know that the people have arrived. I know of the dangers to children, I know of the poisonings; I know of four fatalities since 1984. Two toddlers died in a fire in bed-and-breakfast accommodation. A toddler died early last year, fell over the banisters.

We have a very high rate of TB in this area. I know that there's concern about proper screening, about homeless families' access to GPs. Since we have opened the new Accident and Emergency part of the new wing over here they've been overwhelmed. We think it's homeless families using A and E in lieu of GPs. They're having real difficulty finding out whether people are in homeless accommodation; not everybody wants to say, 'I am homeless.' The Registrar in Community Medicine is trying to do some kind of monitoring, to work out a reasonable way of asking that's not intrusive and is inoffensive, to try and see if that's the case.

I don't know the rate of homelessness in Australia, but I imagine that it's nothing comparable to here. And I do know enough about the health and race policies to say that it's streets ahead of this country. I mean there are interpreters, for a start. We don't have any interpreters. It's shameful what we do not do. You see in Australia the Health Service is based on a right of access, regardless of your colour, your language, your race, your sex. They also have ethnic health workers at all levels, from planning down to community centres with interpreter back-up – and telephone interpreter back-up, if they don't have enough on the ground. We have nothing like that here. In fact, Australians are always aghast when I describe the lack of provision in our district. They're horrified. Well, frankly, I am too.

In 1982 we had 200 homeless families, and now we have well over 2,000. But probably the crisis began in 1979. I think the impact of homelessness started as the housing policies and the employment policies started to hit several years after the change of government. I'm not saying that before that everything had always been hunkydory. My own awareness is from the beginning of the 1980s.

I'm very aware of the growing differentials in health, and they are certainly growing. Housing prices here have rocketed and so therefore the need for public housing is growing. But you get the Government selling it off, and then rate-capping councils and reducing their ability to build public housing.

I don't see any evidence that any of the money raised from selling off council housing is going back into housing. When you look at [the Chancellor's] current budget options – he has all this money – you have to say, well, it's coming because you've been asset-stripping at such an enormous rate since the Government got into office. They've sold off council housing, they've rate-capped councils. At the same time we see that they're starving the Health Service and that there's an urgent need for public housing. I think it's a tragedy. I'm leaving the country, I'm going to get away from it all!

What would I do if I had any power? Well, for a start, instead of building private jacuzzi marinas on the old Harrow Road hospital site, I would have built low-rise public housing for a community housing association. There are some ways in which the Government is right, I have to say. People do want to own their own houses. Low-cost housing, for low-income people – it's low-income people who are losing time and time and time again in every single way. So, low-rise housing which has a feel for families and what families want. Self-managing groups – a liberal idea of people managing their own community housing, with some connection to the Council, but not total control by them. Because I think in some ways councils don't fulfil their obligations quickly enough to do up – or to get rid of the damp –

whatever it is people need. That needs to be decentralised. Actually some Labour councils have done a very good job of decentralising their housing offices, nearer the public housing, so that they can respond more quickly. That needs to be done.

I can't see how the Tories are actually going to manage to run all their service needs if people on low incomes can't afford to live in London. At some stage the crisis is going to hit because they're just going to lose people, like they're losing nurses and teachers.

I find it hard to understand why the D H S S are prepared to pay gigantic amounts for people to live in squalor. I don't know whether the DHSS are monitoring it. Local councils are certainly monitoring it, and they are complaining, but whether it's recognised by the D H S S – I think projects like the Bayswater Project are trying ever so hard to publicise it, and so are Shelter and S H A C. But I don't think the Government want to hear it. They are very concerned to push their home-ownership policy, because they know it's popular with the majority of the population. Homeless people do not have a vote, because they're in between, so they don't count. Local councils are being rate-capped, power's being concentrated at the centre, so in a sense local councils really don't count much either, because the Government has so much control. I don't think that they need to listen. Here's a government committed to selling off council housing in order to encourage private home-ownership. That's fine. But it doesn't recognise the needs of low-income earners. That's an enormous number of people, that's almost up to 50 per cent of the population. Homelessness is not mentioned in the White Paper – on the new Housing Bill – it's not mentioned at all. So the Government haven't acknowledged the problem.

One of the other sad things is that the Government has this thing called 'care in the community', where they're supposedly releasing long-stay psychiatric patients. One of the worries in bed and breakfast is that you get a very wide group of people coming together. There have been women who have been raped there, children who have been abused because they've been playing out in the corridors where they have no supervision. And violence – muggings and robberies. I've never been homeless myself, but what I've read about the experiences of women in particular, but families in general, is pretty horrendous. The statistics on mental illness in women, depression, for example, are increased enormously when you're cooped up in a hotel. When you've got the danger of attack and of your children either being abused or poisoning themselves – all these contribute enormously to tremendous stress. If you were able to talk to G Ps that's what they would say, I'm sure. Also, if you're asking me about the inappropriateness of bed-and-breakfast for mentally frail people and mentally ill and long-stay release patients – the possibilities of abuse of those people are very strong. Properly staffed, properly managed hostel accommodation and half-way houses – that's the answer to that. Proper care in the community. But that's not what's happening now. Adequate accommodation for families which includes the notion of community, of people's real needs for contact with other people, the need for space, the need for safe play space.

In the area where I live, in Notting Hill, there are communal gardens. The housing all backs on to one communal area. Now that is an architectural design feature that seems to me brilliant! Why wasn't it replicated all over London? Not only in the rich areas; it should have been everywhere. That's an enlightened notion. Now if you had, say two or three storeys, and from each storey you had access to the communal playing area, that would be wonderful. That's the kind of accommodation that would be accessible, in income terms, to everybody. With a chance to own it yourself. It would be wonderful.

I was having lunch with a colleague and her visiting friend from Canada. We went walking through the hospital areas and we were joking about Paddington as an area for healing people: here we have a hospital, centralised in what is the most dismal agglomeration of rotting Victorian buildings, where there are no trees, where there are no green areas. One of my colleagues, who's rather more sensitive than most, makes a joke whenever we go out of pointing out the mountains and the lakes. We make up psychic landscapes because this area, as a landscape, is so awful. There is nowhere for the patients to go walking. What do they look out on? They look out on Paddington Station, which is crumbling. They look out on the old St Mary's block which is crumbling. It is not a healthy place for human beings. Okay, there's Hyde Park, but you can't see it from here. They can reach it when they walk through all the hovels, and they can get to it, but they can't see it. The hospital is very poorly located; I would not put a hospital in this area. Whereas St Charles, at the northern end of the district, does have trees, does have gardens. And yet they're going to close it; it's off the regional planners' map. Inside it is built with a real human quality, somebody who knows about human needs, with pictures and paintings, and making somewhere look homely; if you compare it with our new ghastly modern tubular steel building over here – somewhere, the humanity's got lost. We need to build that in.

Mary Tester

Mary Tester is a brisk, efficient woman who runs the Westminster
Homeless Persons' Unit. She is a Londoner in her forties, with a
husky smoker's voice. I met her for the first time in her office near
the Edgware Road, where the interview took place. Mary was
divorced a few years ago, and became homeless as a result.

As a sign of how newsworthy homelessness has become, I was
approached in the waiting room by a beaming, well-dressed man
who asked if it was my first visit. 'I'm just here to do an interview,' I
explained. 'Ah! So am I! Where are you from?' He turned out to be
part of a TV unit filming a programme.

I've worked in housing with Westminster for 16 years, and my career
has progressed to District Officer here. I've been here nearly five years. I
came here as Senior Allocations Officer, after having spent some years
as Senior Officer on the Housing Waiting List. If somebody's registered on the waiting list, they may eventually become homeless. So I had a
lot of background knowledge and experience, if you like, leading up to
a homeless application.

In the time that I was working on the waiting list, we were housing
people on a points basis. So you were saying to people, 'Ah, you're not
off the level yet, you haven't got enough points, but you will have in a
year or two years. So, if you can just stay where you are, you will creep to
that point eventually and we'll be able to help you.'

Today, of course, it's totally different. People aren't being housed on
a points basis. The priority groups are: decant for modernisation,
closing orders and homeless households, and you very rarely get past
those three categories. If you consider that you may have a vacancy, you
must go through the priority order. One of the top priority orders is
going to grab that vacancy, so you would never get down to waiting-list
level, which is about the seventh category down in priority order. If
you're just an ordinary family registered on the waiting list with no
other problems, other than you're in housing need, there is very, very
little chance that you would, today, be housed on a points basis.

The majority of people that come to us – the biggest group of the homeless – are people having to leave the family home. These are Westminster children, who either then have children of their own or get married and live in the parental home. Eventually the parents cannot keep them, so they become homeless, and are priority and will be dealt with through here. These children will have been on the waiting list for many years, and five years ago would have been content to stay in their family home and wait for their turn. But now they're never going to get their turn, and the parents are forced to ask them to leave, so they become homeless.

I don't like to use bed and breakfast, if it can be avoided. I like to feel we use it as a last resort. It's not ideal. It's also very expensive. We try to ask people to stay in the family home – be 'homeless at home' if you like. We'll accept, having either spoken to or written to the parents, that the parents are saying, 'They cannot stay here.' We ask the parents, 'Could you try and keep them, while we do our paperwork?' And then house them directly from the parents' home. I would suggest that we try and avoid bed and breakfast at all cost. You don't have to prove you're homeless by saying, 'Oh, I've got to go into a hotel.' I'm not too familiar with other boroughs. I try not to get too involved with what they are doing. But I would think the most sensible thing to do is to decide whether or not a family's homeless. The question is, are they being forced to leave home? The fact that they may want to leave home wouldn't necessarily mean that I could assist them. I would be saying, 'But you're not being asked to leave home, so you can go back. You're not homeless.' If we think there's a severe overcrowding situation at home, we may not force the girl to stay there. We would try to use our own temporary accommodation, rather than a hotel. Accommodation that I have here, exclusively for homeless households. We've got a variety of small units, single rooms, five houses in W2. I've got flats above this office, we've got another block in Victoria, another block around the corner – so we have got quite a lot of temporary accommodation. We've also got a lot that is managed for us by housing associations. We have got about 260 of our own units.

They are fair-registered rents, so for a large bedsit you would probably be asking a maximum of £25 a week. A two-bedroom flat would be £38 to £48 a week. So there is a considerable saving, costwise. At the moment, my units are treated exactly like council tenancies. Everybody on Social Security is certificated for Housing Benefits, and they are only required to pay a proportion of the amenity charge. If they're working, of course, they're far better off in their own temporary accommodation because of the low rent. Every unit has its own cooking facilities but some are not completely self-contained, so they share showers and baths.

Everybody will be paying more for their accommodation after April [benefit changes], out of their own pockets. They'll be receiving less benefit. The [clothing and furniture] grants that are available now will cease and they will consider – and I mean consider – giving people loans to buy basic furniture. These loans must be repaid from their benefit. Getting a loan will depend whether DHSS feel that, with their reduced entitlement, they will be able to pay. We get a lot of people who become homeless and unemployed at the same time, so therefore they wouldn't qualify for the special loans. We're going to have great problems here. Part of my duty now is to recover the accommodation charges from the clients. I'm strictly monitored. All my temporary accommodation units, from the Director [of Housing]'s point of view, are looked at as recoverable rent. I can't deduct them at source. If a client goes into more than thirteen weeks' arrears and they're claiming Social Security, then I can ask the DHSS to withhold the charge and to pay me an extra £1.60 against the arrears that are on the account. But it's up to the DHSS whether they'll do that or not. If they don't pay we have to take proceedings against the client. If the client disappears then that is dead money. A lot of our clients do disappear.

The fact that Westminster houses a lot of bed-and-breakfast establishments means that we have got a bigger homelessness problem than anyone else, because we have got everybody else's homeless families. I'm quite proud of our figures for bed-and-breakfast. I've got a total of 316 households in bed and breakfast. Now of that, 93 are not in Westminster. They are spread between Dagenham, Streatham, SW5 – all quite near. We managed to find some very, very good bed-and-breakfast establishments, cheaper than in Westminster. In a way, it irritates me that other boroughs don't – if I can find them, why can't they? I think Westminster isn't very popular with other boroughs, because we do take a tough line, or seem to. But I would like to think that we are fair.

It's not satisfactory using bed and breakfast, but there is always a time when you have to use it. I haven't got access to enough alternative accommodation not to. You may have a family with very young children living in a bed and breakfast. They would have access to cooking facilities, but so would everyone else in the hotel. Plus the lack of play space for children . . . it's fine for emergency, short-term, until you can arrange an alternative. But I must say this Council is looking at an awful lot of leasing arrangements with private landlords. We've recently acquired 16, brand-new two-bedroom houses, which we filled within

158

three days. They are absolutely beautiful. I mean, I can see we are going to have problems moving people out of those into their permanent offers. They're in Leytonstone. And at the end of the month, or early April, we're getting another 30 houses around there.

I know it's going to sound hard but I certainly have met people who are intentionally homeless. From my point of view, I think you should be able to use that part of the legislation. I have seen many, many people who give up accommodation elsewhere to come to London – Westminster – to find work. Now these are very sad cases, where people are coming from areas of great unemployment and want to work. They're not aware of the housing problem. Most times we can get their old tenancy back – they've only just left it. So we say, 'Look, thank goodness we've been able to do this, because we aren't going to be able to help you down here. We will offer you the means to return to this area of great unemployment where you've got a home, at least.' A lot of people say, 'No. We don't believe it's hard to find accommodation. We're going to have a look round ourselves.' We stress to them that, in the event of their giving up that accommodation, if they come back, we're going to say that they're intentionally homeless.

You've always got to ask yourself, 'Was it reasonable for the family to have left that accommodation?' If they've got accommodation in another country, and they just decide that they'd like to be here, then I would say it's unreasonable. The biggest group from abroad would be from Bangladesh. Families joining the head of the household. The Immigration Act tells you that a family, or one member of a family, that settled here before 1973 has the right at any time to bring their family to join them. They don't need to provide accommodation, so it is our duty.

This is being tested at the moment by Tower Hamlets. They made the decision that a lot of Bengali families were intentionally homeless, for bringing their families over without providing the accommodation first. So Tower Hamlets are disregarding the Immigration Act. It is a very interesting case, and what was even more interesting was that Tower Hamlets won their decision on the first hearing. The case has gone to appeal, and it's being heard at the moment. So the result of that will certainly affect all boroughs. I think all the other boroughs will follow suit. I would seek advice from my Director, which way he wanted me to go, and if that's the way I was instructed to go, so be it. Then it's the family's decision, what they would want to do – whether they'd all go back, or split up again. Consider that they may have been split for 20, 25 years. But it's not fair to ask somebody who's employed by a local authority, such as myself: 'Do you think that's fair?' I am a paid employee, and if I wasn't happy about carrying out instructions I wouldn't be sitting in this chair. I don't let my personal feelings affect my job. I can separate the two.

I do think it's very difficult even to consider assessing someone in fear of violence as being intentionally homeless. The onus of proof is on the local authority, don't forget. And if you can't disprove it, then surely you should allow the benefit of the doubt. I don't think there's been a case through this office where we have assessed a person in fear of violence as being intentionally homeless. I think that is totally unreasonable.

I can and do identify with the homeless, because I've been homeless, about seven years ago. So I know what it's like, I've been through it. It happened to me by divorce. I think having been through it, I know exactly what the families are going through. It's – not very pleasant. It's a very difficult time in anyone's life.

Why do I think that homelessness has got worse over the last five years? [Firstly,] you've got to look at the availability of accommodation in the private sector. Many years ago or not that many it was very easy. You could rent a bedsit or a flat. With these landlords that you've got now, they can charge exactly what they want, just calling it a holiday let. The property isn't out there.

Second, to be very critical of other boroughs, I think you've got to look at the ones who have got very liberal policies, and accept everyone as being homeless and priority. In an ideal world, yes, of course that should be the case, but it isn't so today. You cannot house everyone that walks through your door. It's not only that more and more people are walking through the door. Over the last couple of years we have seen a lot more new referrals than we've ever seen before. But if you look generally through all the other boroughs, there are more people in bed-and-breakfast now than there ever have been. Is it, though, that more people are approaching the authorities as homeless, or is it that the people that are in bed and breakfast have been there so long that they're not new cases?

From my point of view selling off council flats has only been recent, over the last eight months. I'm sure that has made the homelessness crisis worse. It can't improve it. But on the nicer side, it's a policy that is giving a lot of first-time buyers the opportunity to buy their homes. So there is that as well. All right, it's not too much of a help for homeless households, because I would say the majority of families that we deal with wouldn't be in a position to consider purchasing, even at discount prices. So the only way it would benefit my clients, is if a lot of council tenants in undesignated estates and blocks bought the designated and left the vacancies for me to house people in.

One thing that could be done to improve the lot of people in bed and breakfast, of course, is to look for alternatives. Look to providing more suitable temporary accommodation while you investigate. Don't forget that not everyone that comes through here who is accommodated in bed and breakfast will eventually be housed. But I do feel that bed and breakfast is totally unsuitable, and that every council should be looking to improve on other sorts of temporary accommodation – self-contained units – the way we are trying to do – using the private sector, making more use of housing associations as managers.

We've seen over 3,000 new homeless referrals this year, and that's a lot. We put an awful lot in a bed at night, albeit in the emergency hostels where they don't have a waiting list; you just turn up and it's first come, first served. They queue outside. If a family turns up here and they are priority need, we have a duty to provide temporary accommodation while we investigate. 'Priority' means those with severe medical problems, physical or mental. It means the elderly, and this council accepts that 60 and over is priority. Families with dependent children, or with a pregnant member. Of course, people in fear of violence are priority, but we wouldn't provide accommodation for a single woman, for instance, who was in fear of violence. She would have to have children or be expecting a child.

As a matter of fact, we have been interviewing all our hoteliers over the last two weeks to suggest that they reduce their prices. Well we're not suggesting it, we're saying, 'You must reduce your prices, or we won't use you.' I know other authorities are also doing the same. We've managed so far to achieve between 10 per cent and 15 per cent reduction. It's not good enough. I have accepted it for now, on the understanding that we will be coming back in three months to talk again.

Shelagh Laslett O'Brien

Shelagh, together with Judy and Ahea, runs the three-room Drop-In Centre Playgroup at the Bayswater Families Centre in Cleveland Square, Bayswater. Shelagh is 38, with dark-red hair and green eyes. She lives with her husband, a gardener, and their three children in a housing association house in Earls Court. Because she is lively and funny, the homeless women come to see and talk to her as well as to entertain their children. At the Drop-In Centre – the only place of its kind in the area – women living in the hotels can relax, gossip, smoke and make tea or lunch. The changes in Social Security Shelagh refers to took place in April 1988. Since then the situation of the homeless in London has become even worse, but Shelagh and her colleagues at the Bayswater Project are still struggling to provide help and information.

I was working at a playgroup in Notting Hill Gate, on the fringes of hotel land, and we started to get families coming into the playgroup from the hotels. I could see that they had lots and lots of problems; whereas normally mums would leave their children with us, they wanted to stay and talk about their problems. So I very soon realised what was going on, and I heard that they were trying to set up this group specially for homeless families in Bayswater, and they were having trouble finding someone to do the job. So I was approached and asked if I'd be interested, and I said yes, because I'd been at the playgroup quite a while and I wanted a new challenge. Which it was.

I met Anne Cross, the health visitor, and the vicar, whose hall we began to use, and I was left to get on with it. We started off with a box of toys, a blanket for the babies and a semi-circle of chairs in the hall. This was in January 1984. Initially it started because Anne had identified the problem by talking to these young mums, totally isolated and worried about their children. It was at their instigation that this group was set up. So right from the beginning, it was because they wanted it. We stayed at that place for six months, but we had to move. After that we moved six times, which was quite traumatic, and eventually landed up here. We only had one room at the front, which was very crowded and not really adequate, so we had to fight and fight and fight. Sometimes we had ten families in there, so you can imagine what it was like, but we did it. So having this much space is great, although it's not really adequate at times.

I've always been aware of homelessness. This is different to an ordinary playgroup because you have much more contact with the parents, and also the children tend to be that much more demanding. I prefer this. I think my own experience as a young, isolated mother really brought it home to me that people need more than somewhere to dump their children for two hours. It's all very well doing that, but when it comes down to it if you're an isolated mother at home then you need something else. You need stimulation and to be with other people, you need to use your brain, and you don't really get the opportunity to do that when you're stuck at home with small babies.

I think sometimes the adults get more out of being here than the children. As far as I'm concerned, when they initially come, they're more important than the children. If they're not happy, if they don't feel welcome and settled, then they won't come back, no matter what it might mean to the children. I think some women have come and not particularly liked being with all these women; some people are like that, they're loners, but they've sort of seen it through because they want their children to have the facility. But that's quite rare. I think the mums get just as much out of it as the children do.

I think it helps that I've got three children, so I know what it's like to be up all night with screaming babies – and also to feel broke. I understand when people say they haven't got any money. When my children were small my husband was working away a lot, so for months on end I was virtually a single parent. I really did feel that I needed something more than just being with children. I feel very strongly that during that period when you're at home with children, you lose your identity, and you're frightened, the world out there becomes a frightening place. You think that your brain is no good, or everything's advanced so much that by the time you go back to work you'll be a dummy. Also you forget how to cope with people. The conversation revolves around what you had for dinner, the state of your baby's nappy, what you're feeding them on, soap operas and children's television. It's soul-destroying, it really is. I can really understand these women's urges to have more, I really sympathise with them. And that's why I do everything I can to encourage them to do something else: to go to college, or even do Keep Fit for one hour a week.

Women are always giving to everybody else; it's all output. Unless you go to work, you're not treated as a serious person: you're just someone's mum, somebody's wife, somebody's auntie – and I think that's a waste. There's so much talent, brains, and guts – these women've got so much guts. I really admire them.

It can happen to anybody, ending up in bed and breakfast. There's an awful lot of ignorance about homelessness. I used to think about my job all the time. I had to train myself to cut it off, because I found that every night I was on the phone to someone, or I was sitting at home and typing, reports or something, talking about it or worrying about a particular family. But I had to learn not to do that. I must admit, sometimes I do go home and have a stiff drink. It's very intense.

Quite a few of them do keep in touch when they've been rehoused, the ones that have been long-term do. Or sometimes you get a special kind of person that integrates into the group very quickly. They get a lot out of it, the children get a lot out of it, and they find it hard to let go – you become their friends. We see more of these people than we see of our own families. They do become important to you, I mean I care what happens to them, I care very much. If you see somebody heading towards disaster then it's very hard.

I see our role as a support network, a very important support network. Unfortunately, as I've always said, the families that come here are not always the ones that need us most. They're the ones that are still sitting out there in the hotels with their curtains drawn. It's one of the most depressing aspects of the job. When I used to go round the hotels a lot, at two o'clock in the afternoon you'd find mothers sitting there in their nighties, curtains closed, watching TV. And the kids are always asleep. Two- or three-year-olds, just sleeping. I'm sure it's out of sheer boredom. I've seen depressed two-year-olds, with furrowed brows and all the cares of the world on them. It's awful to see that. I've actually seen rooms without windows, doors that don't open – you can imagine if there was a fire, how awful that would be. Those people are aware of that all the time. Go over and over it again in their minds: what if there was a fire? I can't open this door. There is no window. In one room there was a very, very high ceiling, and there was just a skylight, and it was right at the back of the hotel. Absolutely horrific. The claustrophobia that the people in it must have felt.

What do I think of the bed-and-breakfast system? It's awful. It's a terrible waste of money, and the thing is that all these people don't just lie back and take it. They're all acutely aware of how much money is being wasted. You know, they can all add up. And none of it makes sense. It's mathematical or financial madness. Everyone knows that. A child of six can work it out. I think this adds fuel to the anger that

164

people feel, the desolation. That they could put that money to a much better use.

Obviously the Government want to run down the council-house system. And offload the responsibility on to the private sector. Bit by bit, it's going. What would happen if they rented 500 decent flats at £200 a week and stuck a family in each? That's a great idea. They're doing it, aren't they? But they're only doing it as a temporary measure, because they obviously see £200 a week as too much money.

In actual fact I think the general public would be more alert and angry if they thought people were being put in proper houses and it was costing £200 a week, but they accept the fact that councils can spend £1000 on hotel rooms. It's weird, isn't it? For instance, there was a large family put in a house in a very posh place in Porchester Mews. That was costing £800 a week, and there were letters to the local papers, what a waste of money, but all those thousands of families in bed and breakfast didn't seem to worry them. I suppose it's okay if they're suffering: I think people's image of the homeless is that they put themselves there. They're no-hopers, down-and-outs. People say to me, 'What are you doing there with the homeless families? God, it must be terrible!' They see them all as drug addicts and junkies. When people actually come here, they always remark on how well-dressed the children are, and how pleasant the women are. They find it hard to believe that the homeless could be just like anyone else. So again, it's ignorance.

There's definitely a difference in the children's development. Specially the children that have been in the hotels a long time and just come to us; they're usually very, very behind. We get nine-, ten-month babies that haven't started to crawl, children that don't talk, lots and lots of speech problems. But we do find that if they've been coming for a while, they do actually catch up quite quickly. In fact sometimes they become more advanced because they've had access to these facilities and to lots and lots of people five days a week, which many two-year-olds, say, don't have. They get talked to a lot, there's a lot of stimulation.

I think women have always been landed with their family problems. That's the way it is, that's society. There's plenty of these women that come here have got men, but when it comes to the crunch, getting advice and sorting out the day-to-day family problems, it's the women that are landed with it. The men do tend to go off somewhere; they go and visit their mum or find something to do, and the women are left. A lot of men don't actually see how these women are suffering, being left to deal with it like that. But I think the relationships are under a terrible strain. I can see why they do need to get away from each other during the daytime. To manage to survive under these circumstances is asking an awful lot.

I welcome men here, and we've actually had male volunteers, and they've been great. I wouldn't block it at all, I think it's wonderful. A lot of the children don't have a male around, or maybe the only close relationship they've had has been with a violent man, and I don't think you should protect them from the male of the species because of that. I think it's good to show them that there are gentle, caring men around. And it does work. Not all men would like to come and be here with all these women. They've got to be very understanding men.

The women in the hotels keep themselves to themselves. There's so much fear. I suppose if there's trouble, then they have to live with it. They share the bathrooms, share the kitchens, their kids are annoying each other and the other residents, banging on the doors. In some of the hotels, there are prostitutes living there as well, using them for their business. There are drug addicts, ex-psychiatric patients – you know. And all those are very frightening things. Like for instance, ex-psychiatric patients: it's not just frightening for the families, it's frightening for the psychiatric patients. So I can see why people shut themselves in their room, why they're so glad to get out.

There is one other centre in Bayswater but no one goes there. I feel that when you're setting up something like this, you've got to ask the users or the would-be users what they want. You don't set it up and think, 'Well, they obviously need hygiene classes,' or make it run so that it's easy for you. If it's easy for you then you're probably not doing it properly. If it's hard, then you're probably doing it right. I mean this place looks like chaos most of the time, but it's used. At the end of the day the place is semi-demolished and it's dirty but we don't mind. In a way it's great to see that dirt because it's been well used. Overflowing nappy bucket, overflowing rubbish bin, the carpet's full of crisps and cigarette ends and coffee cups and dirty saucepans, but people have really used it.

Of course, measures could be taken to make homelessness better. It's got worse, obviously, because they've stopped building and they're selling off. Up until the early 1970s there was a building programme, so there was always an element of homelessness, but they were dealing with it. Now they've stopped building, and more and more people are needing homes. Also there's been a drive towards the South – people looking for jobs. I don't know if they've reached a point of no return. They keep telling us how many empty properties there are, how many private properties. But I don't think this private sector thing will work, I think it's a bit of a myth. I dread to think how the new Social Security laws in April [1988] will affect these people. I can just see it putting even more pressure on us. Because the thing is, when it comes to the crunch, it's always the voluntary sector that bails people out. Always. Whenever there's a crisis with money or equipment, whenever their social services or whatever fail, they always come to us. It shouldn't be like that, we shouldn't have to do that. The very fact that we exist is wrong.

We have two grants, from Camden Council and Brent Council, as well as the funding from National Children's Homes. But, because those two councils are under enormous pressure, and overspending like crazy, those grants will probably be cut back as well. N C H took us on more happily because that other money was there. So I don't know how they'll feel about it. They pay our salaries and running costs. There is a plan for us to move eventually, and it would have to be bigger or else I wouldn't go. Well, it isn't up to me, really, but I would resist it. If things do get worse and the numbers are higher, and if the choice was there, I suppose we could keep this place on as well. But I wouldn't like to have anything much bigger than this, and have to accept larger numbers of families, because I think it would break down. I've seen it happen. You get over a certain amount of families, and you're not a group any more, which is not good at all.

As far as this building's concerned, I'd say the optimum number's twenty. That's about what we've got now, which is fine. We haven't had to turn people away yet, and I'd hate to have to. Theoretically, if anyone from Brent comes, we're supposed to send them round to the Brent Centre, and we have done that a couple of times, but they've come back, which is a terrible shame. If they're playgroup age then I would suggest they go to a playgroup but, as I say, the women want something as well. Quite often they want to be with their children, because they feel so vulnerable anyway. Having the children go out of their sight, and the children seeing their mum go out of their sight, is very traumatic for both of them. They tend to want to stick together.

I do enjoy my work. I wouldn't do it if I didn't. I love it, I really love it. I actually get up in the morning and want to come to work . . . I'd done some social work before. My mother-in-law used to run a community settlement. It was a hostel for boys that were in care, or ex-borstal, or ex-lifers. Then they used to run old people's clubs and they had a housing association and they used to give advice. I was a secretary for a bit and obviously, because I was there I was very involved with all the residents. I really enjoyed it. It was great. It made me more aware and much more accepting of people than I was before. You know, when you're young, it's layabouts and hooligans – but when you actually knew what had happened to them and what they'd had to go through, then you could see. It's actually a series of rejections over their life. It's affected how I see an aspect of this job. When a child comes here and is really wild and is maybe a biter or a spitter, that is the first child to get rejected. Not only do they get rejected, the mother gets rejected, and they go off somewhere else and get rejected – and consequently the child's behaviour gets worse and worse, the mother gets more defensive, and it gets serious. They start doing things to get attention, like breaking in, or whatever. So if we get a child like that, we make a special effort not to reject that child or the mother, and to accept them, no matter how hard it is, and I think that's really really important.

It's something that I try to relay to the others, when they say, 'He's really naughty, we can't have him here.' I say, 'No.' I've never turned a child away. We've had some real horrors. Absolute horrors. But it's worth it, because they realise that someone will accept them as they are; even when they do these horrendous things and kick you in the leg you're still going to talk to them and be nice to them. You might be angry at the time but, later, you forgive them. And once they realise that, then they like you, and it changes. Rejection is awful. Working here has made me less selfish, I suppose. I'm very aware of how things can go wrong, very quickly, and it's made me a more careful person. And when I'm presented with 'facts' now I don't just accept them for what they are.

I think all these hotels should be like apartments. They should have their own bathrooms and their own kitchens, no matter how small they are. If possible they should have separate rooms for the mums and the kids, again even if they happen to be small. Maybe they could use platform beds. It's that feeling of space, of privacy and control over their lives. Because if someone else is using the toilet and the bathroom and they're dirty, you've got no control over that situation; your child is exposed to that. If you can't cook, you've got to eat somebody else's cooking, you can't control that, you can't control your child's diet. All these things add up to making these people feel vulnerable. People have said to me, they can't even have a good row with their husbands, they have to whisper! Even when they've put the baby to bed at night, they have to go and sit outside in the corridor for hours. Then someone noisy outside will wake him up – the frustration of that.

The hotels accept the families, accept the money, but they don't accept that families have to be catered for. There's no play facilities, usually no laundry facilities. I feel very strongly that if they did have those things the families wouldn't give them so much bother anyway. People wouldn't be forced to leave their children in their room when they go down to the kitchen, so they get exposed to accidents. Some people have to travel up in lifts with a baby under one arm and a boiling hot saucepan in the other – I've seen some horrific burns because of that. Most of the children that come to this group have been burned. Kettles have either got to be on the floor or somewhere where the children can't reach them. No matter how vigilant and careful parents are, it's very, very difficult. And I think it's totally unacceptable.

What would I do if I had half an hour with Mrs Thatcher? I'd strangle her. I'd like to put her in a b-and-b actually. Put her in the worst, worst place. With small children. I don't think the Government or the councils have any understanding of the situation, not really. I think unless you're actually down there, in it, yourself, or with the people that are in it, you just tend to see it as statistics. It's very easy if you're in a position of power. You just see x number of people who've got to be accommodated for x amount of time; x number of buildings have to be brought into use; it's got to cost x amount of money. But if it was happening to their daughters or their grandchildren, then they would maybe understand more. I heard Lord Ross speaking on the radio the other day and he said – which I thought was great – he had a 31-year-old son who was earning £8,000 a year, and he can't find anywhere to live in London. If he can't afford to buy a place, what hope is there for other people? We couldn't afford to buy a house with the two salaries coming in. There's no way we could afford to buy in London, even with our discount.[1]

I suppose over the next year or two, people are going to be forced to accept flats that aren't habitable, or, even worse, people might get accustomed to living in b-and-b. I've actually seen this: if people are in a decent place with cooking facilities and a bathroom, unfortunately they can become quite comfortable there. When you think about it, you've got no bills to pay, no housework, you've got a telephone but you don't have to pay for the room at all or for anything else. So that actually can become quite okay. You can get used to not having the space.

I've seen that happen. And then when those people have moved they haven't been very happy, because they've got all this responsibility. Specially girls that haven't had that before. They don't know how to pay a bill; maybe they've been living at home with their mum, they've gone into b-and-b, they're still cushioned against all these things, then all of a sudden, maybe for the first time, they are out there, they've got a flat to furnish, bills to pay, and they are totally on their own with that child. It's bloody frightening.

We've done so much to try and inform the public about homelessness. We've done documentaries, we've used ordinary women, ordinary families, lovely-looking children, articulate people, we've shown them the conditions in the hotels, we've shown them how much it costs – how much more can you do? Unfortunately people in this country are a bit smug. If it's not happening to them I don't think they really care. What I've always said is that we've got to keep pushing the fact that this could be your daughter. This could happen to you. Your mortgage could fail. It *is* happening to people with mortgages; the Government seem to be hiding those figures.

Perhaps some people would have chosen not to move to the South if they knew what it was going to be like. There's so many Irish families coming over, I don't know how much they're told over there. But the thing is they're so desperate, because there's just no work, everyone's just leaving, they're either going to America or they're coming over here. You can't blame them for that. I'd do it. Wouldn't we all? Wouldn't those people in the Government do it, or would they be happy to sit in a Liverpool slum and face maybe another 50 years of their life with nothing? Living from hand to mouth and watching their children go through the same? Will people have to say, 'Well, I can't have children because I can't put them through this'? There's nothing, there's no hope.

Lots of people would love to live outside London. I would, but I know that by so doing I'm taking an enormous risk. We actually started looking for a house to buy. We've always lived in Kensington and Chelsea, our schools are there, why shouldn't we? We started looking. Even with a transferable discount of 40 per cent we were looking at houses for £100,000, a three-bedroomed house. So we started looking further and further; we got as far as Cambridge and we came to our senses. If we were in Cambridge would we have work? Probably the answer's no. Do I want to be that far away from my family and friends? No, I don't. But more and more people are faced with that. Why should they be?

Look at Westminster's policy, selling off 50 per cent of their housing stock. Not at prices ordinary people can afford. £50,000 up. So it's not second-generation council tenants that can afford to buy, it's professional people. Big spenders.

People in bed and breakfast *can* vote, if they live here a certain amount of time. It's left to people at the Bayswater Project to broadcast it, find people and tell them, but then by the time they become homeless they're so pissed off with life that they cannot be bloody bothered. They don't believe that anyone's ever going to help them or do anything for them.

I suppose I used to think the Labour Party was wonderful, and everything they stood for. Now I just think they're mostly con artists. They're all there because of a huge ego trip. I don't think they really care. If it was a Labour government, though, I think we would get more. I just think there's so much back-biting and trying to outdo one another, that it's all just got lost. I don't think a Labour government would be as bad as this lot. It's disgusting. They are hard, they are totally hard. Nurseries are being closed down now, playgroups are being closed down, community transport's gone or going, home-helps are almost non-existent. All those things that are vital to people's quality of life, are just being wiped out. At least the Labour Party's going to put that in. I think the Tories are just bloody awful.

My job's definitely getting harder. We're seeing many more people in crisis. Before, over a three-month period, maybe a couple of my mums would have a crisis. But now it's every day. Not receiving money when they should, just for day-to-day living. If you've got a tiny baby to feed, that's really awful. They have to go and spend two days sometimes sitting up at Tresco House, which is an awful place. I reckon the DHSS is collapsing. I'm sure it is. They just can't cope. A lot of the claimants blame the people that work there, but it's not their fault, they are at the mercy of the higher-ups. A lot of people go and work for the DHSS in the hope that they will be able to help people, but they are treated as badly as the claimants. Apparently a huge percentage of them are on Family Income Supplement themselves. The conditions behind the counter are just as bad as out in front, and they refuse to do anything about it.

I've always said, ever since I worked here, I cannot understand how people in b-and-b stand it. When I go in those hotels I just cannot wait to get out. I have babysat and it's awful. I just found it so claustrophobic, and so frightening, I couldn't stay there with my children all night. I've seen fires; we had one woman here who jumped out of a sixth-floor window and broke her back. She had to throw her children out first and then jump herself. That was just around the corner. There was that Clanricarde Gardens disaster; eight people died in that, in 1978 or 1979. There's been awful accidents but you see, we don't get to hear of them all.

There's this respectable façade in Bayswater, isn't there? People think, ah, this is quite a pleasant place, lovely park, beautiful white houses, and behind so many of those doors there is just, awful misery. When I drive down Sussex Gardens now I feel like there's a great grey cloud descends over me. I can't wait to get out. I hate it. I just really feel for those people sitting behind those doors, because I know what's going on. But so many people don't. And you feel so frustrated that you can't do anything. You feel you'd like to liberate all these people, give them a new life. We have tried to organise them as a group to campaign. Apathy sets in, that's why it's important to catch people quickly when they go into a hotel, and get them to come out and do something. Once that apathy and depression gets hold of them, it's very hard to get them out of it, very hard indeed . . .

My dream would be that they all get somewhere to live in the community that they want to live in. A decent flat, where they want to be, where it's warm and clean and they've got neighbours and play areas and schools and they're not frightened to live. They're not frightened to go out. So many people, when they are rehoused, become prisoners, because the community they're put in is so violent, and going downhill so much. I've heard people say, 'Oh, but once you've shut your front door you're all right.' That is cobblers! It's not all right, what's important is what's outside. That's where all your motivation and your satisfaction comes from. You might as well live in a decorated cell, in prison, mightn't you, for all the good it does you? If you can't walk out of your door and go for a nice walk and feel the sun and look at some flowers and watch your children run around, then what sort of life have you got?

It's not just an urban problem, it's happening all over. Some people are being put up in wooden chalets down in Dorset, and in Truro there's a dreadful caravan site. Apparently in winter there's a sea of mud, and they've all got calor gas, and of course the calor gas things blow up because they freeze.

It's legalised abuse by the Government. They've been denied education, health, and they've been denied a proper family life. Look at all the young people in London, our kids. In a few years' time they might meet someone, they might want to start a family – how can they? Unless they go through this sort of misery. Have they got to go through terrible deprivation and live in little boxes to be able to do what we've done? Why shouldn't they be able to enjoy life like that? They can't do it unless they're rich; if you're rich, you can have a family. Then you can live life normally. If you're poor, you can't. So what do we do? We stop having children now, do we? Only the rich can have children. Maybe that's what the Government wants, I don't know.

In April, when it [the changes in Social Security rules] hits them full blast, people are going to be coming here. When they've been to Social Services and been turned away, when they've been down to the Housing Office and been turned away and told the truth, they're going to come here. They've made everything so bloody complicated; if you've got a degree in sociology you might be able to work it out. Ordinary people like me find it very difficult to sort out all this jargon. What about people who can't even speak English, how are they supposed to sort it out? There'll be lots and lots of people going without, because they won't be able to read between the lines, or they don't have anyone to tell them. The people who can tell them are going to be absolutely inundated at a time when grants are being cut. We're just waiting for Camden's decision now on our grant. They want to carry on but I think they're being forced to cut back.

There's got to be some major disaster, like King's Cross. It's sick. That's what we've always said: what do the public need? God forbid, that we need an outbreak of meningitis, or the plague – something awful – I don't know what people need to shake them out of their apathy. How big does the scale need to be? One child dead should be enough, shouldn't it? But it's not: it's got to be hundreds of people dead. People have to have it splashed all over, drama and whatever. It's bloody sad, but I think this has got to happen before people will take notice.

Note

1 There are two kinds of discount available to encourage housing-association tenants to buy. A portable discount is for tenants of charitable housing associations. Under the scheme, these associations can buy dwellings on the market and resell them on 'Right-to-Buy' terms to tenants. Funds from the local authority are limited and payment is discretionary. A transferable discount allows housing-association tenants a sum of money to enable them to buy within the private sector, as a way of equalising rights between housing-association and council tenants.

Afterword

Nobody can have read this book without coming to the conclusion that the current use of bed-and-breakfast accommodation is mad, bad and sad. It makes no sense to politicians of the left or the right and certainly not to the homeless families themselves.

It is essentially the outcome of forced privatisation of housing but is further compounded by the relationship of the homeless to the kind of society in which we now live. Isolation, exploitation, sexual harassment and economic deprivation are sadly not unique to those living in bed-and-breakfast hotels, but the combination of these factors with insecurity about accommodation makes it hard to imagine a more difficult situation for human survival.

The parallels with prison are the most apt, but the only crime these people have committed is their failure to afford accommodation. That puts them in the same financial dilemma as over 50 per cent of the households in London who, on current income levels, could not afford to buy.

There is only one long-term solution to homelessness, and that is to have more affordable homes. It is only through hearing the views of politicians that it is possible to understand why such an obvious solution is difficult to achieve.

Housing – like many other aspects of our lives – has become a lottery. The middle income couple who have bought a second home in France on the benefit of a windfall rise in house prices, and the lower income couple who have just bought their dream bungalow by selling the council house they bought ten years ago, have had a winning ticket. The homeless women interviewed in this book have lost out – perhaps the winners can ignore them – but what about their own sons and daughters who can neither buy nor rent, set up home nor house children of their own?

For there to be a real long-term solution there will have to be a realisation by us all that a lottery is a crazy way to run a housing policy; and that maybe the possibility of hitting the jackpot is just too high a price to pay for all the other people who consequently do not have a home.

A sane housing policy involves us all in making calculations about gains and losses. Politicians' unease about the radical change that is required to solve the problem is based on the fear that you and I will not like it, whatever we might say about the unacceptability of homelessness.

This book is a testament to the price our current housing policies demand of women. It is this that is clearly unacceptable, and we have to persuade both the public and politicians that change is needed now.

Housing is also about social power. When access to housing becomes based almost entirely on income and not on need it is not hard to imagine who loses out. It is the same group that always loses out when individual wealth replaces collective responsibility . . . women. Not all women, of course, but some women more than others. But they lose out because of the fundamental inequality of being a woman.

Social power is also about dividing people into the deserving and undeserving. Racism is another fundamental criterion underpinning the exercise of that power. It is no real surprise that it is shared by some of the homeless themselves.

What is more difficult to face is the fact that we all make these kind of judgments. Do the homeless need to meet our criteria before they have a place they can call home?

But that is in the long term. More immediately, the use of bed and breakfast could be ended in six months if there was a concerted political will. That change is desirable to all those involved, and there are a number of organisations campaigning to achieve this.

There are also a number of organisations trying to improve the quality of life for those currently in bed and breakfast who need help and voluntary support. They all need money, but above all they want people to raise the issue anywhere they have a voice. Change only comes through campaigns with a real breadth of support – those by, for example, Shelter, SHAC, Bayswater Hotel Homeless Project, and the Local Organisations Network comprising local projects such as Earl's Court Bed and Breakfast Project, Tower Hamlets Homeless Families Campaign, Shepherds' Bush Families Centre and Field Lane Homeless Families Centre.

All these organisations depend on the support of individuals. Only by joining forces can we hope to persuade politicans of all parties that a decent, affordable home is a basic right for everyone.

Sheila McKechnie
Director
Shelter
September 1989

Further reading

Audit Commission, *Housing the Homeless: The Local Authority Role*, 1989.

Bayswater Hotel Homelessness Project, *Speaking for Ourselves: Families in Bayswater Bed and Breakfast*, 1987.

Booth, Alan, *Raising the Roof on Housing Myths*, Shelter, 1989.

Burrows, Les, *The Housing Act 1988: A Shelter Guide*, Shelter, 1989.

Conway, Jean (ed.), *Prescription for Poor Health: The Crisis for Homeless Families*, London Food Commission, 1988.

Health Visitors' Association and the British Medical Association, *Health Visiting and Homelessness*, 1989.

London Boroughs Association, *Giving Hope to London's Homeless – The Way Forward*, 1989.

London Housing Unit, *Just Homes: The Equal Opportunity Implications of the Housing Act*, 1988.

London Research Centre, *Access to Housing in London: A report based on the London Housing Survey*, 1988.

Malpass, P. and Murie, A., *Housing Policy and Practice*, second revised edition, Macmillan, 1988.

Matrix, *Making Space: Women and the Man-made Environment*, Pluto, 1984.

National Housing Forum, *A Future for Rented Housing*, National Federation of Housing Associations, 1988.

Niner, Pat, *Homelessness in Nine Local Authorities: case studies of policy and practice*, D O E, 1989.

Resource Information Service, *The Women's Housing Handbook*, 1988.

Thomas, A. and Niner, P., *Living in Temporary Accommodation: A Survey of Homeless People*, D O E, 1989.

Thompson, Lorraine, *An Act of Compromise: an appraisal of the effects of the Housing (Homeless Persons') Act 1977 – ten years on*, S H A C and Shelter, 1988.

Watson, Sophie and Austerberry, Helen, *Housing and Homelessness: a Feminist Perspective*, R K P, 1986.

Organisations

Bayswater Project
Church House, Newton Road, London W2 5LS.

Case-UK (tenants' campaign against sale of estates)
5th Floor, 103 Portland Street, Manchester M1 6DF.

Campaign for Homes in Central London
5 Dryden Street, London WC2 9NW. 01 829 8350

London Housing Unit
Berkshire House, 168–173 High Holborn, London WC1V 7AA.

SHAC (The London Housing Aid Centre)
189a Old Brompton Road, London SW5. 01 373 7841

Shelter
88 Old Street, London EC1U 9HU. 01 253 0202

Tower Hamlets Homeless Families Campaign
Brady Centre, Hanbury Street, London E1. 01 375 2413

Resources

Further reading

Health Visiting and Homelessness, report by the Health Visitors' Association and the British Medical Association, £2.00 from:
Health Visitors' Association, 50 Southwark Street, London EC1 1VN.
Prescription for Poor Health, £5.95 from: Shelter, 88 Old Street, London EC1U 9HU. 01-253 0202.
Speaking for Ourselves, £2.50 from: The Bayswater Project, Church House, Newton Road, London W2 5LS.

Organisations

Case-UK Campaign against sale of estates.
5th Floor, 103 Portland Street, Manchester M1 6DF.
London Housing Unit
Berkshire House, 168–173 High Holborn, London WC1V 7AA.
Tower Hamlets Homeless Families Campaign
192 Brady Centre, Hanbury Street, London E1. 01-375 2413.
Housing Rights Campaign
5 Cromer Street, London WC1H 8LS.

Wendy Webster
Not a Man to Match Her
A Feminist View of Britain's First Woman Prime Minister

Housewife, 'queen', grandmother, warrior, star, soldier, governess, romantic heroine, nanny, iron lady, Britannia, Boadicea, headmistress.

Margaret Thatcher has been constructed, invented, described and analysed, not to say satirised and jeered at during the ten years of her premiership. But never before has she been subjected to a full feminist analysis.

Wendy Webster's acidly illuminating book traces Mrs Thatcher's packaging from housewife to superstar to 'queen'. She examines the two Thatchers, one demurely paraded among women, the other only to men. And she exposes the parody of machismo that not only triumphs over men, but rejoices in humiliating them.

This at last is the *woman's* book about Thatcher, that looks relentlessly behind the designer image. It is the book that angry and bewildered women in Thatcher's Britain have been waiting for.

Politics/Women's Studies   £6.95
ISBN 0 7043 4231 6

Elizabeth Kemf
Month of Pure Light
The Regreening of Vietnam

In 1975, the Vietnam war was over. It had cost the lives of nearly two million Vietnamese. In thirty years of conflict, the people and the landscape had been subjected to many of the latest techniques in modern warfare. Arguably, the result was 'ecocide': the permanent devastation of the country's fragile human and natural environment.

Ten years later, naturalist Elizabeth Kemf first visited Vietnam to observe the long-term effects of the war, and the slow work of rehabilitating the land. In visits over the next five years, she travelled the length of the country, going to areas normally closed to foreigners. The result is a unique eyewitness account of devastation and renewal. Laboriously, and with inadequate resources, the Vietnamese are replanting rain forests and rescuing abandoned terrain for crops. The land is slowly being healed.

Elizabeth Kemf is editor of the international newspaper of WWF – World Wide Fund for Nature. She was consultant on the recent Channel 4/National Geographic Explorer film, *Vietnam: After the Fire*, which was based on this book and was recently broadcast in Britain, the USA and Canada.

Ecology/Peace   £16.95
ISBN 0 7043 5050 5 Hardcover

Angela Y Davis
Women, Culture and Politics

'Behold the heart and mind of Angela Davis: open, relentless, and on time! She is as radiant, she is as true, as that invincible sunrise she means means means to advance with all of the faith and all of the grace of her entirely devoted life' June Jordan

In this resounding new collection of essays, lectures and other writings, Angela Davis deals once more, as in her best-selling *Women, Race and Class*, with the issues of the day. Her insight and passion come to bear on subjects ranging from prisons to the Pentagon, the dilemmas of women in Egypt to those of children under apartheid, and her particular vision illuminates the future for us all.

Politics/Women's Studies   £6.95
ISBN 0 7043 4216 2